ONE GOD
ONE LORD
ONE SPIRIT

*On the Explication of
the Apostolic Faith Today*

EDITED BY HANS-GEORG LINK

Faith and Order Paper No. 139

WCC PUBLICATIONS, GENEVA

The texts "Fullness of Faith" (Link), "We Believe in One Lord Jesus Christ" (Ritschl), and "The Prophetic Spirit" (Link), were translated from the German by the WCC Language Service.

Cover photo: Peter Williams

ISBN 2-8254-0906-5

© 1988 World Council of Churches, 150 route de Ferney, 1211 Geneva 20, Switzerland

Typeset by Macmillan India Ltd., Bangalore 25
Printed in Switzerland

ONE GOD
ONE LORD
ONE SPIRIT

In gratitude to

LUKAS VISCHER

on the occasion of his 60th birthday

Table of Contents

Table of Contents

Preface

How do ecumenical statements actually come into being? Is it not important for their assessment to have a certain idea of the several steps within a complex dialogue process which lead to the formulation of ecumenical reports and declarations? This is why we have developed this volume, as a first attempt to glimpse into the "workshop" of the Faith and Order Commission of the World Council of Churches.

In this book we present the initial stages of the elaboration of a common ecumenical explication of the Creed of Nicea-Constantinople of 381. This explication forms a central part of our study "Towards the Common Expression of the Apostolic Faith Today". Other publications related to this study are: *The Roots of Our Common Faith: Faith in the Scriptures and in the Early Church* (ed. by H.G. Link); *Apostolic Faith Today: a Handbook for Study* (ed. by H.G. Link); and the four volumes of the series *Confessing Our Faith Around the World* (all published by the WCC, Geneva).

This volume is dedicated to *Lukas Vischer*, director of the Faith and Order Commission from 1966 to 1979, on the occasion of his 60th birthday. It is an expression of our gratitude for the formative and lasting contributions which Lukas Vischer has rendered to Faith and Order with his great theological and conceptual gifts and his untiring energy in the service of the unity of Christ's church.

We are grateful to the compilers of this volume who had to struggle with an unusual and difficult task. Our thanks are also due to our colleagues in the WCC Publications, the Faith and Order Secretariat and the Language Service of the WCC.

Geneva, June 1987   GÜNTHER GASSMANN
                                     Director, Faith and Order Commission

The Ecumenical Creed

Text of 381 A.D.

We believe in one God,
  the Father, the Almighty,
  maker of heaven and earth,
  of all that is, seen and unseen.

We believe in one Lord, Jesus Christ,
  the only Son of God,
  eternally begotten of the Father,
  Light from Light,
  true God from true God,
  begotten, not made,
  of one Being with the Father.
  Through him all things were made.
  For us men and for our salvation
    he came down from heaven:
  by the power of the Holy Spirit
    he became incarnate from the Virgin Mary,
    and was made man.
  For our sake he was crucified under Pontius Pilate;
    he suffered death and was buried.
    On the third day he rose again
     in accordance with the scriptures;
    he ascended into heaven
     and is seated at the right hand of the Father.
  He will come again in glory to judge the living and the dead,
    and his kingdom will have no end.

We believe in the Holy Spirit,
  the Lord, the giver of life,
  who proceeds from the Father.
  With the Father and the Son he is worshipped and glorified.
  He has spoken through the Prophets.
  We believe in one holy catholic and apostolic Church.
  We acknowledge one baptism for the forgiveness of sins.
  We look for the resurrection of the dead,
    and the life of the world to come. Amen.

Fullness of Faith

The Process of an Ecumenical Explication of the Apostolic Faith

HANS-GEORG LINK

An *ecumenical explication* of the apostolic faith aims at a worldwide agreement on the contents of the Christian faith. It is intended as a contribution to the reflection of all Christians on the foundations of their common faith and as an *interpretative* contemporary presentation of the rich heritage of Christianity, a contribution in *ecumenical* breadth and depth. Its breadth depends on the participation in this explication of Christians — lay and expert, women and men — from all parts of the world. Its depth is reflected in its three-step process: the creed of the ancient church, the biblical foundation, the contemporary presentation. In this way the fullness of the common substantive faith is to find expression in all its breadth, length, height and depth (cf. Eph. 3:18). The way "towards a common expression of the apostolic faith today" begins, therefore, with a comprehensive reflection on what is central to the faith, from which fresh light is thrown on its effects in every corner of the globe.

I. Earlier stages

At its meeting in Crete in April 1984, the Standing Commission on Faith and Order decided to begin its detailed work on the study project "Towards the Common Expression of the Apostolic Faith Today" by undertaking an explication of the Christian faith as presented in the Nicene Creed.[1] The question to be answered here is "to what degree and in which form the main thrust of the three articles of the Creed can, in the wider context of the apostolic faith, be commonly understood and expressed by churches of different confessional identity and living in different cultural, social, political and religious contexts".[2]

In the winter of 1984/85, as a *first* step in this process, three international consultations were held in different continents, with about twenty participants in each case, to combine the explication of the contents of the Creed with regional standpoints and contemporary challenges. Each of the consultations adopted the same procedure: a first stage, consisting of a basic presentation and a regional comment on each main theme, followed by detailed discussion in plenary; a second stage in which three working groups produced initial draft interpretations which were finalized in plenary sessions.

The first consultation was held in the Malankara Syrian Orthodox Church Seminary in *Kottayam*, Kerala, South India, from 14 to 22 November 1984. It began work on the explication of the second article of the Creed: "We believe in one Lord Jesus Christ." Consultation members made the acquaintance of a situation in which Christians are in a minority, in a country where the overwhelming majority of the population is of the Hindu religion. The mystery of the incarnation of the one God, the sufferings of Christ in relation to the misery and hunger of millions of human beings, and the inspiring hope of resurrection against a background of various kinds of fatalism — these were some of the aspects shown up in a special light in the Indian context.

The second consultation, held in the La Fontaine Cultural Centre in *Chantilly*, France, from 3 to 10 January 1985, tackled the third article of the Creed: "We believe in the Holy Spirit . . . the church . . . and the life of the world to come." Here, the themes which emerged as of special importance for the European context included the creative diversity of charisms, the stumbling block of divided churches, and forebodings about the future.

The third consultation took place in the Roman Catholic Nganda Retreat Centre in *Kinshasa*, Zaire, from 14 to 22 March 1985, and tackled the explication of the first article of the Creed: "We believe in one God . . . " In Kinshasa, members of the consultation gained first-hand experience of the strength of the young churches. In this context, there was special emphasis on joy in creation, power structures inside and outside the churches, and the conflict between Christians and Muslims over the Trinitarian view of the one God.

These three consultations in different parts of the world undoubtedly helped to ensure the combination of vertical and horizontal standpoints in the explication of the apostolic faith from the very beginning. Since each of the three consultations produced its own draft explication, a complete first version of an ecumenical explication of the apostolic faith was already in existence at the conclusion of this first round of meetings (*Draft 1*: Kottayam report, Chantilly report, Kinshasa report).

This first version of the explication was harmonized, expanded and annotated in a *second* series of consultations from April to August 1985. First, a small editorial committee, composed of representatives of the consultations and staff of the Geneva secretariat, met in Le Cénacle, a Roman Catholic conference centre in *Geneva*, from 9 to 11 April 1985, mainly for the purpose of standardizing the structure of the three consultation reports (*Draft 2*: Geneva revision). Next, the ten-member international steering group for the study project on the apostolic faith met in the *Crêt-Bérard* Reformed Retreat House near Lausanne from 28 May to 1 June 1985, to revise and supplement the contents of the draft interpretation (*Draft 3*: Crêt-Bérard draft). This version was then sent to all members of the Faith and Order Commission in *Stavanger*, Norway, where it was examined in three working groups — one for each article of the creed. These groups formulated their agreement and criticisms in three *group reports* which were presented and discussed in plenary and finally passed on to the Standing Commission for further revision.[3]

After a much-needed pause for breath, a *third* round of meetings was held from March to July 1986. Firstly, the five executive staff members of the Faith and Order Secretariat met in *Crêt-Bérard* from 17 to 21 March 1986 and at Le Cénacle, *Geneva* on 17 and 18 April 1986, to revise the draft text of the explication in the light of the Stavanger group reports (*Draft 4*: Crêt-Bérard/Geneva revision). Then the international steering group met in *Berlin* (West) from 9 to 12 July and immediately afterwards, from 13 to 19 July 1986 in *Potsdam* (GDR), along with the Standing Commission, to produce the latest provisional version (*Draft 5*: Berlin/Potsdam Explication).

The earlier stages of the work on an ecumenical explication of the apostolic faith may therefore be summarized as follows:

> *Draft 1*: (a) Second Article, 14–22 November 1984, in Kottayam, S. India
> (b) Third Article, 3–10 January 1985, in Chantilly, France
> (c) First Article, 14–22 March 1985, in Kinshasa, Zaire
> *Draft 2*: 9–11 April 1985, in Geneva, Switzerland
> *Draft 3*: 28 May–1 June 1985, in Crêt-Bérard, Switzerland
> *Draft 4*: 17–21 March 1986, in Crêt-Bérard, Switzerland
> 17–18 April 1986, in Geneva, Switzerland
> *Draft 5*: 9–12 July 1986, in Berlin (West), FRG
> 13–19 July 1986, in Potsdam, GDR

Over 150 people from all parts of the world have participated in the almost two years' work (November 1984 to July 1986) so far devoted to an "ecumenical explication" of the apostolic faith. In addition, local groups and study circles have responded to the invitation of the Geneva secretariat to study questions related to the apostolic faith.[4] Needless to say, work has continued on the revision of the draft. The Standing Commission of Faith and Order decided in August 1987 that a preliminary version of the text would be published as a study document.

Three more international conferences are planned for 1987/1988 to deal with certain problem areas of special importance in connection with the ecumenical explication of the apostolic faith, e.g. atheism, Mariology, ecclesiology. Between now and its next major conference in 1989, the Commission expects to have advanced the study project far enough to be able to present its findings at that time officially to the churches.

II. The role of the Nicene Creed (381)

There is no denying the fact that the Nicene Creed has an important role to play in this ecumenical explication of the apostolic faith. This has occasionally led to the mistaken idea, especially in Protestant circles, that the entire project is really no more than a study of the Nicene Creed. More serious still, some of our dialogue partners have voiced the fear that the Faith and Order Commission is retreating into the fortresses of the fourth century in order to deal with the doctrinal problems of the twentieth century. To counter such misinterpretations it will be helpful to describe here as precisely as possible the role of the Nicene Creed in this ecumenical study project.

First of all, we recall the *sub-title* of the present study: "An Ecumenical Explication of the Apostolic Faith as Expressed in the Nicene-Constantinopolitan Creed (381)". A clear distinction is made here between the apostolic faith on the one hand, and its expression in the Nicene Creed. The connection between them is indicated by the word "as". How is this "as" to be understood? Not in a normative sense ("to the same extent that") but *factually*, i.e. as that faith has found actual historical expression in the Nicene Creed. What is meant, therefore, by the guiding role assigned to the Nicene Creed in the ecumenical explication of the apostolic faith is primarily the recognition of an ecumenical fact.

This basic decision in favour of the Nicene Creed has implications for both the content and the method of the ecumenical explication of the apostolic faith.

In respect of *content*: the Nicene Creed serves as a guide to the key themes to be discussed. As a fourth-century summary of the apostolic faith it suggests the list of themes and at the same time limits it. This selective and limiting function of the

Nicene Creed has already proved helpful in the ecumenical explication of the apostolic faith, in face of the vast range of possible themes from which to make a choice. Indeed, it has proved to be the only possible solution to this problem. This does not automatically exclude the possibility of going beyond this canon of themes, as happens in respect of Jesus' proclamation of the kingdom of God, but this will only be possible in compelling cases. When the Nicene Creed is described in the introduction to the ecumenical explication of the apostolic faith as a "basis", what is meant is its role as a guide to the contents of this explication.

In respect of *method*: here the Creed of 381 provides the starting point for interpretation. It is in this sense that it is described in the introduction as a "methodological tool". Its pithy and familiar clauses facilitate access (*met-hodos*) to the apostolic faith. Starting from the text of the Nicene Creed is the first of three systematic steps; it is followed by the second, more detailed in most cases, i.e. indication of the biblical foundation; these first two steps lead on to the third, the explication for today, which is decisive both in content and comprehensiveness.

At the same time, this definition of the role of the Nicene Creed for the content and method of the ecumenical interpretation of the apostolic faith also implies *limitations*. The Nicene Creed is *not* the only touchstone nor is it an absolute criterion for the content of the apostolic faith. This is clear from the fact that its substantive assertions are in every case examined in the light of the witness of the biblical documents and focused as sharply as possible on the questions of our time. In this ecumenical explication, the Creed of 381 has its proper role and function as a relative, time-conditioned and context-conditioned *regula fidei* (rule of faith).

Even in respect of this limited role, it may well be asked why such a key function should be assigned to the Nicene Creed in particular and not for instance to the Apostles' Creed or to some modern creed or confession? Various reasons have been decisive here. Firstly, the Nicene Creed is the oldest of the three ancient church creeds; it stands closest to the original sources. Secondly, it represents an exemplary summary of the basic contents of the apostolic faith, of a sort which we do not even find in the New Testament itself. Thirdly, it is a Creed which was adopted by the Second Ecumenical Council — the faith of the 150 fathers — and it carries the authority of an ecumenical council recognized by almost all the churches. Fourthly, this Creed has proved its value as a rule of faith for millions of Christians throughout the centuries who have struggled and suffered for it and died with its words on their lips. Fifthly and finally, the Nicene Creed is recognized by all the main Christian traditions and continues even today to be by far the most widely used creed among Christians.

In appealing to the Nicene Creed as a guide to contents and as a methodological starting point, this ecumenical explication of the apostolic faith confronts at least the Reformation and post-Reformation churches with the task of looking beyond the Reformation of the sixteenth century and reflecting more seriously and intensively on the ancient church heritage common to all Christians. At the same time, the Western church's Apostles' Creed, though less widely used, is also taken into account in the explication in the hope that it may also find a home in the Eastern church tradition. In the last analysis, however, both ancient church creeds perform their limited function only in connection with the variety of biblical testimonies and contemporary questionings. In this ecumenical explication of the apostolic faith, the ancient church creeds, the biblical foundations and the contemporary interpretations are not to be treated as rivals competing with one another but on the contrary must together find a common voice.

If the Nicene Creed were to find a firm place in the eucharistic celebrations of the western church and the Apostles' Creed a firm place in the baptismal services of the eastern church, that would be a wonderful fruit of ecumenical reflection on the common heritage from the ancient church.

III. Features of this ecumenical explication of the apostolic faith

Ecumenical texts are developing increasingly into a distinctive literary genre. Occasion, place, time, author, theme, conditions — in a word, the whole context in and out of which they emerge — play in them a disproportionately important role. This has been the case since the modern ecumenical movement started at the beginning of this century. To begin with there were *reports* in which participants in ecumenical conferences tried to capture their experiences, discoveries and questions. Then came joint *statements* on theological, ecclesiological and political themes. In 1948 a *basis* was formulated for the World Council of Churches for the first time; in 1961 this was expanded to its present form. In Lima in 1982 a *convergence statement* first saw the light of ecumenical day. Now we are working on an ecumenical *explication* of the apostolic faith.

What confronts us in all these ecumenical texts is a new form of theological literature in which the teething troubles of its early years are frequently only too obvious. What they lack most is the maturity of conciliar texts and they are often contemporary snapshots rather than long-term projections pointing to the future. They are, on the one hand, recognizably the products of a young movement. Fully to understand the language and intentions of its written statements, one has to be a participant in this movement. On the other hand, from the 1948/1961 Basis via the convergence statement of 1982 down to the present explication, there is an unmistakable movement in the direction of more far-reaching statements with ecumenical validity.

It has become plain from the reception process of the convergence statements on baptism, eucharist and ministry how difficult many people find it to grasp the character of this new ecumenical genre, especially if, as in most cases, they have not been involved in its production. In order to facilitate understanding for the "ecumenical explication of the apostolic faith", let me list a few of its characteristic features.

On the whole, the following *five guiding principles* as they are listed in the introduction have proved to be useful in the work of interpreting the apostolic faith ecumenically:

1. The explication deals with *essential* aspects of the faith following the basic affirmations of the ancient creeds. This will leave room for more detailed interpretation, application and implementation according to the respective Christian traditions and cultural contexts.
2. The explication seeks to discover and formulate *common* insights which can be understood and accepted by Christians from different traditions.
3. The explication does not pretend to solve all theological differences. It rather seeks to interpret the apostolic faith as the basic foundation of Christian thinking and life of our *present* time. This includes facing contemporary challenges to the Christian faith.
4. The explication tries to meet the requirements of today by showing as clearly as possible the link between *doctrinal* affirmations and *ethical* problems.
5. The explication attempts to make necessary "*clarifications*" of the apostolic faith in critical response to certain developments of our time.

In detail, the following *eight features* call for emphasis:

1. The ecumenical explication of the apostolic faith takes place in a *process* which requires years and perhaps even decades. The version presented here is only its first fruits and in no sense its final product. The purpose of publishing it is to involve as *early* as possible as *many* as possible of those who are interested in this process of comprehensive reflection on common foundations of faith. As explication, this ecumenical process is in principle unending even if one day it will in fact provisionally end. It is the ambition of this ecumenical explication of the apostolic faith to persuade as many participants as possible to accompany it on the way to the re-formation of Christian faith and life, and it is, as a matter of principle, open to new interpretative standpoints.

2. This ecumenical explication is a *common effort* in which far more than a hundred theologians and laity inside and outside the Faith and Order Commission have already shared. Contributions have been made to this explication from all the main Christian traditions, from the non-Chalcedonian churches to the so-called non-credal churches, and of course, including the Roman Catholic tradition. Points of view representative of all regions of the earth have been expressed and digested. To this extent it is an ecumenically *representative* interpretation. The weight it carries is not derived, however, from any formal authority of any kind but solely from the wisdom it contains and the conviction it carries in its own right, as is the case with other ecumenical documents.[5]

3. The participation of many confessional and regional representatives is reflected in a *multiplicity* of views. But what we have here is no pallid lowest common denominator. Quite the contrary. An effort has been made to achieve the highest possible degree of agreed knowledge. The only effect of the limiting function of an explication for which joint responsibility is assumed is that nothing has been formulated which could not be accepted by a tradition or region. Apart from that, the principle followed by the explication has been to expound the fullness of ecumenical knowledge of the faith.

4. Each of the main Christian traditions has contributed its distinctive *emphasis* to the explication: the Orthodox tradition, the guideline of the Nicene Creed; the Roman Catholic tradition, clarifications from doctrinal developments in the ancient church and subsequently; the Protestant churches, the basic biblical foundations. Our common task of interpreting the apostolic faith for our times received the benefit of all three emphases. To a certain extent, the *structure* of the explication — creed, Bible, today — takes these different emphases into account. The explication has thereby gained generally in tension and depth.

5. In any ecumenical explication it is natural for the different participants to emphasize what *unites* them. The explication then helps people to recognize that, in respect of the substance of the Christian faith, what the churches have in common outweighs what divides them. In an explication in which many persons cooperate in this way, what unites them has necessarily to be formulated at a certain *basic* level. But this is something altogether different from a pallid generalization which exhausts itself in empty turns of phrase. Characteristic of the basic linguistic form is a spaciousness in which different concrete adaptations have their place. This ecumenical explication of the apostolic faith allows "room for more detailed interpretation, application and implementation according to the respective Christian traditions and cultural contexts", as the first of the five guiding principles requires.

6. This raises the question of the relationship of fundamental doctrinal statements to concrete *ethical* applications. The fourth of the guiding principles insists

that the connection between them be shown "as clearly as possible". This becomes all the more urgent since ethical questions today play an incomparably more important role in individual, social, political and economic matters than ever before but also because differences on ethical questions sometimes divide the churches more than their doctrinal differences. Much work is still needed on the explication before it really does justice to the many challenges of the present time. But fundamental limits to its actual ethical applications are also set by different church and regional traditions. These limits may only be overcome, indeed, if the ethical approaches indicated here are developed independently in the different regions and confessions.

7. This is not a theological convergence document like that on baptism, eucharist and ministry. Its primary purpose is not so much to settle individual points of conflict between the churches as to *present* the apostolic faith "in all its rich diversity" as a common ecumenical basis in *contemporary* terms. In a certain sense, it contradicts the very nature of an explication to make any endorsement of its explanations obligatory. The purpose of the explanations, on the contrary, is to engender pleasure at the ecumenical concern for the contents and consequences of the apostolic faith and to point the way to an ecumenical reformation in head and members. To regard them as obligatory doctrinal statements would be to misunderstand them completely.

8. It could be helpful here to remember that this is only the *first* step in the project "towards the common expression of the apostolic faith today". With a future common confession of the apostolic faith in prospect, there is a great deal to be said for *summarizing* later the basic biblical, historical and contemporary approaches of this explication in short concluding paragraphs. These could form the substance of a future convergence text on the apostolic faith aiming at universal agreement.

IV. Suggestions for future emphases

From what has already been said, it is clear that the ecumenical explication of the apostolic faith is only in its initial stages and has certainly not yet found final shape either in form or content. As the Faith and Order Commission secretary entrusted with responsibility for the advancement of the study project on the apostolic faith from 1980 to 1986, I would like now to indicate *five aspects* to which sufficient attention has not yet been given in the work to date. The purpose of these reflections, of course, is to help to ensure an even more comprehensive and relevant expression of the apostolic faith.[6]

1. Our approach to the ecumenical interpretation of the apostolic faith must be broad enough and deep enough to embrace also the *Old Testament and Jewish* tradition of faith, without which as a foundation no agreement on the Christian faith can be complete. Thus already in Rome in 1983 it was affirmed: "We are convinced that the relation of the Church and Jewish people is an essential aspect of the apostolic faith, and that any convergence document must deal adequately with this relation."[7] Encouraging exegetical and systematic theological efforts to include this dimension have already been made in the work on the ecumenical explication so far. To give due weight to our Old Testament and Jewish heritage seems to me of special importance at three points:

a) In emphasizing the *one* God, the one Lord, the one church, the Nicene Creed adopts the fundamental Old Testament confession of the uniqueness of the God of Israel. After a long period in Christian theology in which attention has concentrated mainly on the different persons of the Trinity—almost to the point of tritheism—it is high time today to put the emphasis, as the Old Testament does, on the oneness of God and on the implications of this for the people of God. In Rome in 1983, Michael Wyschogrod, the Jewish theologian from New York, made this statement: " . . . Christian literature on the triune nature of God is far larger than that on his oneness. Can it be that the time has come to investigate more deeply the oneness as well as the threeness of God in Christian teaching? It cannot be expected that the oneness thus developed will be uninfluenced by the threeness but perhaps a better balance between the two doctrines will be found."[8]

b) The *incarnation* of the Son of God as confessed by the Nicene Creed embraces not only his general humanity but also has its full force in the *Jewish* context (family, people, geography and tradition) in which Jesus of Nazareth lived and died. God's incarnation in the Jew Jesus is "a light for revelation to the gentiles and for glory to thy people Israel" (Luke 2:32). In confessing our faith in the divine incarnation, therefore, we give thanks to God the Father not just for the incarnation of his Son as a human being in general but also for the glory of the "peculiar people" from which the light has gone forth to lighten the Gentiles.

c) Finally, confession of faith in the Holy Spirit "who has spoken through the prophets" has implications for the relationship between the *church and Israel*. Karl Barth described this always difficult relationship as "the one really vital ecumenical question".[9] The relationship between the Catholic Church and the Jewish people having been put on a new footing by the Declaration *Nostra Aetate* at the Second Vatican Council[10] and a clear sign having been given by Pope John Paul II with his recent visit to a synagogue in Rome, the time has also come for the member churches of the World Council of Churches to examine their relationship to people of the Jewish faith and to put this relationship on a solid theological basis: the one people of God of both Jews and Gentiles.

2. So far the ecumenical explication of the apostolic faith has taken in all parts of the Creed in roughly equal measure. In future, closer attention is to be paid to the *themes which divide the churches*. For the real ecumenical task of the Faith and Order Commission is to deal with the theological difficulties which have helped to divide the churches in the past. In the light of the fundamentals summarized in the Nicene Creed, there are, it seems to me, three such themes which still divide the churches: the role of the Virgin Mary, the problem of the *filioque*, and the catholicity of the church.

a) In reaction against a usually exaggerated *Mariology* and exaggerated forms of Marian piety in Roman Catholicism, most of the Protestant churches have gone to the opposite extreme of not venturing to say anything about Mary at all. It cannot be ignored, however, that Miriam has her firm place in the Old Testament just as Mary has hers in the New Testament and in the ancient church creeds. It is time for all Christians to discover and define this place. Feminist liberation in Latin America and in Europe has for some time now been on the track of the hidden revolutionary encouragements in the biblical portrait of Mary to put an end to a patriarchalism with Christian trimmings and a tyranny camouflaged as religion. It is high time for Protestantism to rediscover Mary.

b) The *filioque conflict* between the Eastern church and the Western church was examined in detail by the Faith and Order Commission in 1978/79 and the Commission approved the Klingenthal memorandum on this question[11], though this has so far found no echo worth speaking of in the churches. In the context of the interpretation of the third article of the Creed, we need, I believe, to differentiate much more clearly between the Christological legitimacy (I do *not* say necessity) and canonical illegitimacy of the addition "and from the Son" to the procession of the Spirit from the Father. This would allow the churches of the West, on the one hand, to emphasize the ultimate and complete resting of the Spirit on the Son, yet at the same time, on the other hand, to return to the original wording of the Creed. Without such an official step towards reconciliation with the Eastern church tradition, the Orthodox churches can hardly be expected to welcome the Western Apostles' Creed into their church tradition and still less to accept new ecumenical statements of faith.

c) What is most urgently needed today is , it seems to me, the development of an ecumenical *ecclesiology* which allows room for the different church traditions which have developed over the centuries. The main offence in church history has not been the differences between the churches as such but their absolutization accompanied by the condemnation of other churches. The days are over, thank God, when one church claimed to be exclusively the one true and catholic church. What we need today is an ecumenical explication of the marks of the church which links unity not with uniformity, but with conciliar fellowship, and catholicity not with "Romanity" but with the rich diversity of the body of Christ. Equally important, on the other hand, is the overcoming of sectarian particularism and Protestant provincialism, if there is to be any ecumenical renewal of the confession of faith in the one, holy, catholic and apostolic church.

3. One of the specific tasks assumed by this ecumenical explication of the apostolic faith was to examine and, as far as possible, respond to "*contemporary challenges* to the Christian faith" (cf. the third of the five guiding principles). The individual chapters also begin by listing in greater or less detail the relevant issues. But the "explication for today" in each case still seems to me to have gone in most respects too far in the direction of consonance and apologetics. To give one example: when it comes to the confession of faith in the One Creator of heaven and earth and its interpretation for today, it is not just our understanding of heaven and earth but also our practical dealings with them which are challenged. One of the working groups in Stavanger 1985 launched on an examination of "the integrity of creation in light of the apostolic faith".[12] In doing so, it at least indicated the direction to be taken — and taken substantially further than so far — for progress to be made today in the ecumenical exegesis of the apostolic faith. The burning issues of our day must, in fact, be related to the essential content of the Christian faith and the *ethical* consequences of the *fundamental* credal clauses must be drawn. Great strides forward would be made in this ecumenical interpretation if it could for instance also manage to relate confession of the lordship of the Risen Christ or of the future of the kingdom of God to the experiences of daily life.

4. Since 1983, we have made various attempts to involve *local and regional* groups in the work, though only with modest success so far. Down to the plenary meeting in Stavanger, only 15 responses from groups had been received, mostly from Europe, none from Africa, Asia or Latin America. This raises the question how much real interest is taken in this theme and the study of it to date and how far does it meet a felt-need in the different parts of the world. For undoubtedly the comprehensive and fundamental character of this enterprise also sets limits to it.

Would it help if the work of the Commission at world level were to be supplemented by *regional statements on doctrinal questions*?[13] For some years now we have been collecting such statements and can clearly recognize their contemporary contextual relevance, at least at certain flashpoints such as Central America,

South Africa or South Korea. In my view, it would be a real enrichment of the present work on basic questions of faith at the international level if the national Christian councils and regional church conferences (such as the Conference of European Churches) were to adopt the theme and produce appropriate statements, perhaps under the general title of "Challenges and Opportunities for Confessing the Apostolic Faith in Our Part of the World".

5. The substantial work on the study of the apostolic faith has so far concentrated almost exclusively on its central part, the explication, and, for good reasons, this will continue to be so for the foreseeable future. Since a possible bridge to a common credal *confession* was envisaged in the conclusion of the previous section (III,8), I would like now, in bringing this present section to a close, to raise the question of the connection with the common *recognition* of the apostolic faith. Since Lausanne 1927 a number of attempts have been made to establish a written account of what all Christians are already able to agree in accepting. The first of these attempts stated: "Notwithstanding the differences in doctrine among us, we are united in a common Christian faith which is proclaimed in the holy scriptures and is witnessed to and safeguarded in the ecumenical creed commonly called the Nicene, and in the Apostles' Creed, which faith is continuously confirmed in the spiritual experience of the church of Christ."[14] Similar and even fuller statements could be cited from the world conferences on Faith and Order in Edinburgh 1937, Lund 1952, and Montreal 1963.[15] The problem is that, up to now, none of these declarations acknowledging our common Christian heritage has been officially accepted by any Assembly of the World Council of Churches. Nor have any of the more recent declarations, such as "A Common Account of Hope" (1978), "The *Filioque* Clause in Ecumenical Perspective" (1979), or "Baptism, Eucharist and Ministry" (1982).

When we trace the distant beginnings of joint declarations as developed by the Faith and Order Commission, we come across the "Lambeth Quadrilateral" which was formulated almost a century ago, in 1888, as the basis of the Anglican Communion. The question I ask is whether the time has not now arrived, one century later, for an *ecumenical quadrilateral*, possibly along the following lines:

> We, the official representatives of our churches, meeting together at this ecumenical event, recognize, despite the doctrinal differences which still remain between us, our unity in the one apostolic faith
> — as witnessed to in the scriptures of the Old and New Testaments;
> — as summarized in the ancient church creeds, the Nicene-Constantinopolitan Creed of 381 and the Apostles' Creed;
> — as celebrated in the church's liturgy, i.e. in the eucharist; and
> — as interpreted by the ecumenical councils of the church.

If the member churches of the World Council were officially to adopt such a statement at one of the forthcoming Assemblies, this would undoubtedly provide a solid basis for surmounting the doctrinal differences that still remain.[16] We should not underestimate the importance of such an explicit official recognition of our common Christian heritage — especially for relationships with the Orthodox and Roman Catholic traditions. Of course, a formal recognition of this kind cannot and should not be regarded as a substitute for the reappropriation of the content; it can nevertheless serve as a platform solid enough to bear the weight of a reinterpretation and contemporary confession of our common Christian faith.

V. The contents of the book

We publish in this book the *first drafts* of an ecumenical explication of the apostolic faith as produced at the Kottayam, Chantilly and Kinshasa consultations. Differences in respect of the membership and location of these consultations are reflected in the length, exegetical methods and style of these drafts. To a greater extent than later revisions, they reveal the contexts and questions which lay behind the initial approach to the ecumenical interpretation of the apostolic faith.

To provide readers with some insight into this initial ecumenical situation and starting point, and to show them the course the explication has since taken, three participants have provided profiles of the drafting process in terms of selected themes. These profiles are to be taken as reports of ecumenical work-in-progress and intentionally underline the character of this publication as a workbook. Their function is to act as a guide to help the reader to follow, at least to some extent, the vicissitudes of the ecumenical explication in its different stages down to the form it has now reached. This could only be done by selected examples, given the wealth of the themes developed and the limited space available in this book.

We publish these first drafts of an ecumenical explication of the apostolic faith in the hope that this theme will find as wide an audience as have the convergence documents on baptism, eucharist and ministry. We invite as many groups as possible, working groups, pastors' conferences, and such like associations, to examine receptively, critically and creatively the themes touched on here. The Geneva Faith and Order secretariat invites both positive and negative comments, for consideration in the subsequent work of explication. We wish all readers of this book much joy in the rich heritage of our common apostolic faith.

NOTES

1. The title "Nicene Creed" is used for simplicity's sake; the reference is always to the text of the Nicene-Constantinopolitan Creed of 381.
2. Minutes of the Meeting of the Standing Commission of Faith and Order, Crete 1984, *Faith and Order Paper No. 121*, Geneva, WCC, 1984, p.15.
3. Cf. my report "We believe in Father, Son and Holy Spirit", the Stavanger discussion on the proposed ecumenical explication of the apostolic faith today, in T.F. Best ed., "Faith and Renewal: Reports and Documents of the Commission on Faith and Order, Stavanger 1985", *Faith and Order Paper No. 131*, Geneva, WCC, 1986, pp.127ff.
4. On this cf. the "Proposals and Questions for Study Groups on Apostolic Faith Today", in "Apostolic Faith Today: a Handbook for Study", H.-G. Link ed., *Faith and Order Paper No. 124*, Geneva, WCC, 1985, pp.278–280.
5. Cf. the corresponding formulation of the so-called "Toronto Statement", "The Church, the Churches and the World Council of Churches" (1950), in L. Vischer ed., *A Documentary History of the Faith and Order Movement 1927–1963*, St Louis, Missouri, 1963, pp.167ff.
6. A written version of these reflections was in the hands of the members of the Standing Commission on 19 July 1986 in Potsdam: Theological Considerations on the Development of the Apostolic Faith Study.
7. "The Roots of Our Common Faith: Faith in the Scriptures and in the Early Church", H.-G. Link ed., *Faith and Order Paper No. 119*, Geneva, WCC, 1984, p.18.
8. *Op. cit.*, p.31.
9. In C.A. Rijk, "Das gemeinsame Band. Die Bedeutung der christlich-jüdischen Beziehung für die Einheit der Kirche" (The Common Bond: the Significance of the Christian–Jewish Relationship for the Unity of Church), in *Bibel und Kirche*, 1974, p.44.

10. In Austin P. Flannery ed., *Documents of Vatican II*, pp.738–742.
11. "The *Filioque* Clause in Ecumenical Perspective", in "Spirit of God, Spirit of Christ: Ecumenical Reflections on the *Filioque* Controversy", L. Vischer ed., *Faith and Order Paper No. 103*, Geneva, WCC, 1981, pp.3–18. "Apostolic Faith Today", *op. cit.*, pp.231–244.
12. In "Faith and Renewal", *op. cit.*, pp.146ff.
13. Cf. the series "Confessing Our Faith Around the World", I–IV, *Faith and Order Papers 104, 120, 123, 126,* 1980–1985.
14. "The Church's Common Confession of Faith", report of Section IV of the Lausanne conference 1927, in L. Vischer ed., *A Documentary History of the Faith and Order Movement, op. cit.*, p.33. "Apostolic Faith Today", *op. cit.*, p.69.
15. "Apostolic Faith Today", *op. cit.*, under the heading of the several conferences.
16. It would be a remarkable ecumenical gesture if, during its commemoration of the centenary of the Lambeth Quadrilateral in 1988, the assembled bishops of the Anglican Communion were to take the initiative in proposing such a step.

PART I

The First Article

We Believe in One God
An Ecumenical Explication

Report of a Faith and Order Consultation held at Kinshasa,
Zaire, 14–22 March 1985

A. The one God
    I. The theme
    II. The Creed
    III. The biblical witness
    IV. Today

B. The Father Almighty
    I. The theme

    a) God the Father

    II. The Creed
    III. The biblical witness
    IV. Today

    b) The Almighty

    II. The Creed
    III. The biblical witness
    IV. Today

    c) Conclusion: the Father Almighty

C. The Creator and his creation
    I. The theme
    II. The Creed
    III. The biblical witness
    IV. Today
        a) The Triune God as the Creator
        b) The Creator acts — in redemption and revelation
        c) God's good creation — and evil

  d) Humanity in creation
  e) Consequences
    1) Humanity's mandate over nature and the destruction of our environment
    2) Human responsibility in a world sanctified by the Triune God

A. THE ONE GOD

I. THE THEME

1. In the world, "there are many 'gods' and many 'lords'" (1 Cor. 8:5). Phenomenologically speaking, a god is an object of worship, prayer, and trust; it is what constitutes for an individual or a group their ultimate value. At its best, religion is the serious and sincere search for the good and for fullness of life. Human sinfulness, however, introduces distortions that lead to idolatry, this being finally the magnification of self (Rom. 1:19ff.; Phil. 3:19).

"Where your heart is, there is your god" (Luther, Large Catechism). In this sense, there are no atheists. On the other hand, there are atheists in the sense of those who consider that *belief in God*, far from being the way of life and salvation, is rather a threat to the freedom and dignity of humankind; belief in God would rather be an illusion springing from psychological, sociological or economic grounds. In the early centuries, Christians were accused of atheism because they abandoned the pagan gods. Contemporary atheism may today be challenging believers to purify their notion of God.

In face of the problems of existence in our world, some people are unable to find any transcendent or ultimate reference in life. Some of these place their hope for betterment in humankind itself. Others have abandoned the quest in a nihilistic way.

2. Many peoples and several religions profess faith in a single, universal god, the creator, sustainer and goal of everything else that is. That transcendent god gives meaning and worth to created reality. The crucial question concerns *the identity of the one God*. Christians believe that "the one true God", who made himself known to Israel, has revealed himself supremely in "the one whom he has sent", namely Jesus Christ (John 17:3); that, in Christ, God has reconciled the world to himself (2 Cor. 5:19); and that, by his Holy Spirit, God is bringing new and eternal life to all who through Christ put their trust in him.

3. For many religious people outside the Christian community, *the notion of the Triune God* has been a stumbling-block. Either it threatened monotheism as they conceived it; or, in the other direction, it excluded their own more multiple perceptions of the divine. Even within the church, many people today consider that the Christian doctrine of the Triune God stands in need of fresh interpretation and terminological revision. It may be that the work of clarifying the Christian doctrine of God both for those outside the church and for those within will best proceed hand in hand.

II. THE CREED

4. The Nicene Creed confesses belief in *one* God, *one* Lord, *one* church, *one* baptism. The foundation for all authentic ecclesial and human unity is the one God: "There is one body and one Spirit, just as you were called to the one hope

that belongs to your call, one Lord, one faith, one baptism, one God and Father of us all, who is above all and through all and in all" (Eph. 4:4–6).

5. From their Jewish heritage Christians have known since the start that "there is no God but one" (1 Cor. 8:4). The church of the second century affirmed against Marcion the *unity* of the God who creates and redeems. It took time before the church gave a fully reasoned account of the relation between the "one God, the Father, from whom are all things and for whom we exist" and the "one Lord, Jesus Christ, through whom are all things and through whom we exist" (1 Cor. 8:6). The determinative moment came with the Arian controversy. While Arius held that the axiomatic unity of God could be maintained only at the expense of Christ, the Nicenes believed that the Christ who was worshipped as Lord, and in whom salvation was given, belonged essentially to the Godhead. The Council of Nicea (325) affirmed the Son to be *homoousios tō Patri*, understood as *ek tēs ousias tou Patros*. After a subsequent and similar controversy, the Council of Constantinople (381) declared also the lordship of the Holy Spirit, "who proceeds from the Father and who with the Father and the Son together is worshipped and glorified". In all this, the church had no sense of destroying the unity of God; rather the one God, on the basis of his redemptive activity in history, was understood as Triune. Baptism continued to take place in the single name of Father, Son, and Holy Spirit.

6. In the development of Trinitarian theology, a *tension* has existed between those who found the unity of God upon the divine essence which would, as it were, underlie all three persons, and those who see in the Father the personal "source of deity". The latter view would appear to be closer to the original Nicene formulation (although *ek tēs ousias tou Patros* was not taken up into the creed with which we are dogmatically and liturgically familiar), and it is particularly characteristic of the Cappadocian fathers and the Eastern churches. The Western churches, following Augustine, tend in the former direction. Recent thinking on the *koinonia* of the Godhead may, as we shall see, suggest a reconciliation between these views, which belong in any case more to speculative theology than to the fundamental confession of the faith. In both East and West, doxological language confesses both the unity of God and the distinction of persons with equal insistence; and it is in worship that the personal character of the Triune God is most apparent.

7. There is no easy access to the *understanding* of the credal formulas. Although the word *homoousios* itself was subject to a multiplicity of possible interpretations, the general concern of the early church was to guarantee the oneness of God and to secure, therefore, the unity of the three divine Persons. Nicene theology thus stressed at the same time the individuality of each of the three hypostases of the one God who reveals himself throughout the history of salvation, *and* the dimension of communion (*koinonia*) in the one divine being. Today care needs to be taken with such words as "substance" (which now often suggests material, subject to instrumental measurement), "essence" (which may recall a discredited metaphysic) or "person" (which may evoke an individual subject, an atomistic centre of consciousness). It is also necessary to show how the relation between 3 and 1 is not merely arithmetical. It remains an urgent task for the church to develop together a contemporary terminology explicating for today the precise meaning of the formulas of antiquity.

III. THE BIBLICAL WITNESS

8. The Councils of Nicea and Constantinople sought to ground their teaching in the scriptures. Biblically, the true God is "the living God". Genesis begins with the

first act of God *ad extra* in the creation of the world, which remains the object of his interest and affection, the "theatre of his glory" (Calvin). *Israel* had learnt to know this creator God in his redemptive history with them. In his dealings with his elect people Israel, God is known as YHWH, the Lord. It is the Lord who brought Israel out of Egpyt, and on that account he alone is entitled to the people's worship; all idols are therefore to be rejected: "I am the Lord your God, who brought you out of the land of Egypt, out of the house of bondage. You shall have no other gods before me. You shall not make for yourself a graven image, or any likeness of anything that is in heaven above, or that is in the earth beneath, or that is in the water under the earth; you shall not bow down to them or serve them; for I the Lord your God am a jealous God" (Ex. 20:2–5a).

In the promised land, a centuries-long struggle was needed before Israel, always threatened by apostasy, won its way, at least as a remnant, to accept the exclusive claims of the Lord over the gods of the land. The prophetic witness was especially important in this regard. The Deuteronomist declares the faith of Israel: "Hear, O Israel, the Lord is our God, the Lord alone. You shall love the Lord your God with all your heart, all your soul, and all your might" (Deut. 6:4f.). The greatest clarity concerning the uniqueness of the Lord and the all-encompassing extent of his sovereignty was — miraculously — attained at the time of most severe testing: it is in Second Isaiah, prophet of the Babylonian exile, that Yahweh is acclaimed as universal creator and as redeemer of Israel: "There is no other god besides me; a righteous God and Saviour; there is none besides me. Turn to me, and be saved, all the ends of the earth; for I am God, and there is no other." (Isa. 45:21–22).

9. *Jesus* affirmed the faith of Israel concerning the one God. He dismissed Satan by citing the scripture: "You shall worship the Lord your God, and him only shall you serve" (Matt. 4:10; cf. Deut. 6:13). He endorsed the "Hear, O Israel" as the first and great commandment and the way to eternal life (Mark 12:29; Matt. 22:37; Luke 10:27). The God of Israel called Jesus his Son (Luke 1:32; 3:22 = Matt. 4:17). Jesus addresses this God as "Father", using the intimate word "Abba" (Mark 14:36), etc. Jesus is the Father's own, beloved, the only Son (John 1:18; 3:16; Rom. 8:32; Col. 1:13). Whoever has seen the Son has seen the Father (John 14:9), for the Father and the Son are "one" (John 10:30). While remaining distinct, the Father and the Son "dwell" in each other (John 17:21). At the prayer of the exalted Christ, the Father sends the Holy Spirit into the world, to be for believers "the other Paradise", the Spirit who "makes alive" and guides into all the truth.

IV. TODAY

10. The *one* God reveals himself as a *communion* of life and love. The progressive revelation of the Trinity in the New Testament coincides with God's self-communication to humanity. The Father makes a radical gift of himself through the incarnation of his eternal Son, who shares the human condition even to the point of death, in order to offer to humanity the resurrection and eternal life (John 3:16). The life of the incarnate Son, as the total gift of self to God and to his fellow human beings, reveals that in God himself, life is mutual self-giving and communion. All that is summed up in the declaration "God is love" (1 John 4:8). The cross of Christ is a revelation in history of the kenotic love of God which gives itself in order that life may be manifested as fullness of communion. The cross cannot be understood apart from the Trinity, nor the Trinity apart from the cross. Without the God who is love, the cross is both scandal and foolishness, just as the doctrine of the Trinity, without the cross, remains intellectual acrobatics, if not an absurd-

ity. As the emblem of the incarnation, death and resurrection of the Son of God become man, the cross is the affirmation of a love which is stronger than sin and death. This love which reveals itself in the history of salvation is the God who is both one and Triune. If God reveals and communicates himself as love, it is because he first of all is in himself love and koinonia.

The fullness of the biblical revelation consists precisely in the fact that the one God is an eternal communion of life. The eternal source of that living communion is God the Father, who eternally begets the only Son (John 1:1, 18) and eternally breathes out the Holy Spirit (John 15:26). This does not mean that the one God is divided, but rather that life in God is the free gift of self in communion. The eternal communion of life reveals itself *ad extra* as the Creator of the world (Gen. 1:1, 2:4; Ps. 33:6; John 1:1–3), as the world's Redeemer, and its Sanctifier, its beginning and its end. The work of each Person of the Trinity implies the presence and cooperation of all three.

That the Creator of the world and of humankind is this eternal communion of life and love is what gives the world a meaning and a purpose. Created in the image of this eternal communion of life and love, humankind has as its final end the vocation to become ever more truly the image of the Trinitarian communion, reflecting and witnessing to the active presence of the Trinitarian love in the world.

11. The Triune God is the source and model of *the church's life*. According to John 17:21, the mutual indwelling of Father and Son (*perichoresis*) is the source, model and locus for the unity of the disciples of Jesus: "that they may all be one, even as thou, Father, art in me, and I in thee, that they may also be in us . . . " To a monadic God would correspond a monolithic unity of the creatures. Christian unity is rather that of a free fellowship in love, the "communion of the Holy Spirit" (2 Cor. 13:13); its concreteness and visibility rests upon the word made flesh, into whose body believers are integrated as members. It is the one God, Lord and Spirit who is the source of all the varied gifts, which are to be harmoniously directed towards the common good (1 Cor. 12:4–7).

The unity of the Trinity, both as the perfect unity of the distinct Persons and as the mutual indwelling of the Persons, is revealed in scripture as the only unity that the church is to manifest in its life "in order that the world may believe" (John 17:21). This unity transcends all unity of a purely logical or arithmetical kind: it is a unity of koinonia. Both the unity and the difference of the divine Persons are of equal value in the constitution and manifestation of koinonia. Trinitarian unity, therefore, is the negation of all subordinationism and the refusal of all isolationism, separation or indifference towards others. Each divine Person lives the life of the others, and each divine Person lives not only with the others (co-existence) but also for the others (pro-existence). Local churches united in the image of the Trinitarian koinonia will each live the life of the others, and all will live the life of each, while yet keeping their specific gifts. The same faith and spiritual life is the content of each, and of all together. This Trinitarian koinonia ensures both unity and the liberty of each and of all, in such a way that the unity never becomes subordination or totalitarianism, and the liberty never becomes isolation or selfish individualism. Thus the life of the church and the churches will bear witness among humanity to the mystery of the God who is love.

The pattern of "conciliar fellowship" to which the churches are called today should be a reflection of this Trinitarian life. It should allow a more transparent manifestation of the communion of life and love that Christians have with God the Trinity, amid a world marked by sin, divisions, injustice, and lack of communion.

That implies more fraternity and solidarity in and among the Christian communities, more collegiality at the structural level, more collaboration in diakonia.

12. Christian faith in the one God who reveals himself as a supreme communion of life and love has profound significance not only for the life of the church but also for the church's engagement in the *service of the world*.

Faith in the *one God*, Creator, Saviour and Judge of the world, should always inspire refusal of every human effort to replace the true god by false gods created in the image of absolutized selfish passions (the desire to possess, to dominate, to destroy, to deceive). At the same time, faith in the one God should never serve as the pretext for actions contrary to the will of God as this is expressed in the commandments of love towards the neighbour; invocation of the one God can never sanction injustice or oppression.

Faith in the one God who is supreme *communion* of life and love should inspire Christians to grasp, encourage and sustain all efforts towards justice, peace and respect for persons or peoples marginalized, oppressed, threatened by suffering, sin and death, or any form of life that is not authentic communion.

If the world is regarded in the light of faith in the Trinity, then every aspiration towards justice, peace, the sharing of resources, the democratic distribution of power, the freedom of persons and peoples, can be perceived as a conscious or unconscious aspiration to live in the image of the supreme communion of life and love, in which humankind was created (Gen. 1:26) and which mysteriously beckons to human beings in various and ever new ways at every moment and period of history.

That is why the search for visible Christian unity cannot be undertaken without the interest of the churches in the renewal of the human community, a renewal permanently desired and sustained by the one God.

13. Whereas polytheisms present a plethora of unrelated or warring divinities, the oneness of God — Father, Son, and Holy Spirit — offers the coherence of all created reality, at least in the final kingdom, when all sin and disruption will have been overcome and "God will be all in all" (1 Cor. 15:24–28). This Christian doctrine of God also provides a *framework* for locating those *semina Verbi* which are the signs of the presence and activity of the one God "who is not far from each one of us, for 'in him we live and move and have our being'" (Acts 17:27–28). What others still "worship as unknown" the church now proclaims (17:23) when it preaches the Saviour whom God has appointed to judge the world (cf. 17:30–31). This is none other than the Jesus who is "the way, the truth, and the life", our access to the Father (John 14:6).

14. Belief in *one* God (monotheism) is a shared patrimony of several religious traditions, notably *Christianity, Judaism, Islam*, and even *African traditional religion*. Whereas the first three, said to be religions of the "Book", base their belief on an explicit revelation, African traditional religion derives its belief rather from a spontaneous intuition of a being, who must be behind the entire created order, as its primary source and ultimate foundation.

Christians are sensitive to the fact that the other monotheistic traditions do not share their faith in a Triune God and indeed often accuse Christians either of polytheism (Islam) or idolatry (Judaism).

In answering the accusation of *polytheism*, it is important to stress that, historically, no Christian writer of note (whether "orthodox" or "heretic") has ever been known to espouse tritheism. If anything, the over-riding concern in all known Trinitarian controversies has been to preserve the unity of God intact.

Nevertheless, whereas the Christian belief in a Triune God is the affirmation of a God who is koinonia and, therefore, personal, the Islamic affirmation is rather of a God who is an absolute and eternal solitude. Such a God does not communicate his very self to humanity nor invite humanity to enter into communion with himself. Christians profess faith in a God, who is love (1 John 4:8). The others believe in a God who is absolute will. With such a God there can be no communion as Christians understand that word.

The root of the Judaic accusations of *idolatry* lies in the incarnation, and only then addresses the Trinity. If the incarnation is a fable or a mere myth, then, indeed, it would be idolatrous to adore and worship Christ. But the Old Testament is as much the Book of Judaism as it is of Christianity. The same Old Testament abounds in prophecies of an age in which God himself would erupt into human history, and be "Immanuel" ("God with us") (Isa. 7:14). If, as every Jew fervently believes, God's word is never sterile, but always accomplishes what it promises, then the incarnation is entirely a possibility. Christians believe that the Old Testament prophecies have been realized in Christ, and that, therefore, the incarnation of God has found its fulfilment in him. In him, God's word — in the dual sense of "logos" and promise — has taken flesh: the Logos has become incarnate and the promise has found historical realization. Therefore, Christians do not consider it idolatrous to profess faith in Christ as God, and to adore and worship him as such, always within the context of the Trinitarian faith.

So far as *African* traditional believers are concerned, they would wish for a justification of the Christian faith in a God who is both three and one, without being polytheistic or "diffusely monotheistic", as some have described the African traditional type of monotheism. The difficulty encountered here could be resolved in an eventual dialogue between both faiths: Christianity and African traditional religion.

For the rest, notwithstanding the apparently insurmountable differences between the various monotheistic traditions, the door should be open for dialogue between them. Such dialogue, carried out in an atmosphere of openness to divine guidance and inspiration, can be expected to bear fruits of greater mutual understanding and mutual respect among the various traditions. We may all come to see new things in our own tradition.

Note: For their better understanding, many in the church today are seeking clarification concerning the doctrine of the Triune God. Needed, in the first place, is a greater appreciation of the issues at stake in the early centuries, so that the scope and importance can be seen of the conciliar decisions taken concerning the truth of the faith and the marks of Christian identity. Without an awareness of this historical background, the summary formulas risk either being reduced to mere badges of orthodoxy for parrot-like repetition or else rejected without yet being understood. The hallowed formulas of the early church are best kept alive in the liturgy and theology of the church when they are expounded in preaching that draws upon the whole scriptural history of salvation and seeks to make the message intelligible to contemporary men and women.

B. THE FATHER ALMIGHTY

I. THE THEME

1. The Creed goes on to identify the one God more specifically as "Father Almighty". Much else that might also be affirmed concerning the being and nature

of God — his eternity, wisdom, goodness, faithfulness and so on — is implicitly included in this *personal name*, which lies at the heart of the first article as the fundamental characterization of the God in whom we believe. It gives the preceding description, "One God", substantive content, and leads on to the following words, "Maker of heaven and earth . . .", which draw out further one main dimension of its meaning.

2. At the same time, to call God "Father Almighty" already points forward to the second article and to the uniquely-begotten Son. This makes clear that the Father is supremely *Father of the Son*; that "one God" cannot properly be taken as referring only to the Father in isolation but directs us instead to the undivided Trinity of Father, Son, and Holy Spirit; and, in general, that the first article does not stand alone but is followed by and integrally related to the second and third. In this sense, to affirm the one God as Father Almighty is to denote the ultimate theological foundation of everything else in the Creed. There is therefore every reason for this study to consider with care what this affirmation expresses, how it may be open to distortion and misunderstanding, and its bearing on the contemporary articulation of our common faith. With this aim in view, the following sections will deal in turn with the terms "Father" and "Almighty".

> *Commentary*: The name "Father Almighty" may be analyzed grammatically in two ways according to whether "Almighty" is treated as a substantive in apposition to "Father" ("the Father, the Almighty") or in a more adjectival sense ("the Father Almighty"). The wording of the Ecumenical Creed can be taken in either sense, and both interpretations have been common in the history of the church. Each has its place. The first invites us to consider the distinct meanings of "Father" and "Almighty", the second to attend to the force of their conjunction, in particular to the mutual qualification of "Father" by "Almighty" and "Almighty" by "Father".

3. This analytical reflection is all the more necessary because the description of God as "Father Almighty" is often employed with little consideration of the original sense of the words, of the content and range of their meaning, or of their relation to the rest of the Creed. That way lie serious dangers. The specifically Christian sense of the first article may be lost from view; one-sidedly authoritarian, paternalistic and triumphalistic associations may consciously or unconsciously colour its interpretation; these in turn may call forth protests and objections, issuing sometimes in rejection of the entire Christian faith. Such objections have indeed been directed against both "Father" and "Almighty" as suitable descriptions of God. They challenge us today to consider such *questions* as:

— Can the fatherhood of God properly be understood in a non-patriarchal and non-authoritarian way?
— Does "feminine" as well as "masculine" imagery have a necessary place in inclusive theological language? And, if so, can we go on to address God as "Our Mother" as well as "Our Father"?
— In what sense do we affirm that God is the Father "Almighty"?
— What is the relation or resemblance between the sovereign power of God and the "powers" at work in the world?
— What are the similarities and differences between the Christian affirmation of the Father Almighty and comparable expressions used in other religions?

a) God the Father

II. THE CREED

4. The confession of belief in God as *Father* undoubtedly carried with it belief in God as creator of the whole universe. In the second and third centuries this was a dominant theme in Christian writings. God is Father by virtue of his being Creator of all things. This was underlined in the first article of the Creed by the close association of "Father" with "Creator of heaven and earth". Belief in the fatherhood of God as creator of all is a belief shared not only by Hellenistic Judaism and the Greek world of the early centuries, but is common in the belief of many religious peoples including African traditional religions.

5. The description of God as Father in the Ecumenical Creed bears a further and yet profounder meaning: the Father is *Father of "Jesus Christ*, the uniquely-begotten Son of God". The relation of the Father to *this* Son, of *this* Son to the Father, is the axis on which the Nicene confession of faith turns. Arius had held that the Son did not share the being and nature of the Father, but was, rather, his primal creation, who might be described as "begotten" or "made" or "created" or "established", but who at any rate was not divine as the Father is divine. Against Arius, the Creed witnessed that Jesus Christ is uniquely and distinctively Son of the Father ("begotten, not made"), eternally one with the Father ("of one substance with the Father") and fully God ("Light of Light, true God of true God"). The Council of Constantinople, in the final formulation of the Ecumenical Creed, added that the Holy Spirit "proceeds from the Father".

6. The close association of Creator and Almighty with Father in the opening statement of the Creed tended to underline the idea that *dominion* and *authority* belong to the fatherhood of God. The Father God is the one who rules and wields authority over all creation. Too great an emphasis on these aspects of fatherhood, particularly in the Greek world of the early centuries, easily led to the distortion of the notion of fatherhood. It helped to produce an all-powerful, impassible absolute deity, more a cause or principle than a person, thus overshadowing the personal dimension contained in the word Father itself.

7. However, belief in the fatherhood of God, as it is confessed in the first article of the Creed, was understood as referring particularly to the special relationship between the First and Second Persons of the Trinity. The Father is Father of the Son. The name Father belongs to God in virtue of his relation to the Son, Jesus Christ. The use of the word father was common in the *religions* of the Ancient Near East, often with *biological* and sexual connotations where an ancestor of a tribe was thought to have had a god as his father or where the earth's fertility was closely connected with its divine impregnation. The Greek myths told of marriages between the gods and mortal women and the birth of heroes.

8. In contradistinction to these, *Christian belief* in the fatherhood of God was never intended to imply that God is male. "It is important to note that when the Creed speaks of 'Father' and 'Son' in their relation to each other in the Trinity, it does not mean to imply that God is male. As a human being, Jesus Christ is male. But within the persons of the Trinity, there is no gender" (Kottayam report, p.9). Although the biological metaphor of begetting is used for the eternal relationship between the Father and the Son, the describing of Christ as the *only*-begotten of the Father not only indicates the uniqueness of this relationship but also its *otherness* from any human begetting. Moreover, the words "God from God, Light from Light" made clear that the begetting of the Son by the Father was not to be

understood in terms of human begetting. God the Father could never be seen as a quasi-male, a human-like sexual father.

9. The statement of belief in the fatherhood of God was, further, understood only in that unique relationship between Father and Son seen in the life, death and resurrection of Jesus of Nazareth. The fatherhood of God is grasped in relation to the centrality of the *cross and resurrection*. The Father is known most fully as Father loving the world, when he allows his Son to be crucified (John 3:16). At the same time the Son knows what it is to be Son when, in obedience to the Father's will, he shows his love for the Father in bearing the suffering of the cross, dereliction and death. In response to the love and obedience of his Son, the Father gives himself in the power of the Spirit to the crucified Son by raising him from the dead. The cross is inseparable from the resurrection. When Jesus surrendered in Gethsemane and on the cross and was raised from the dead, the true meaning of fatherhood as it is confessed of God, the Father of the Son, Jesus Christ, is most truly apprehended. Although the Son alone was crucified, the Father participated mysteriously in the suffering on account of his love for the Son. It was in his love that the Father abandoned Jesus to death on the cross and in his love that he raised him from death to live. In the death, resurrection and ascension of the Son the Father shares all the power and glory with his Son. Here God gives proof of a radical difference from the all-powerful and impassible Father, and from the misconceptions of human fatherhood which have distorted and limited the image of God.

10. Nor was it only the second article of the Creed that gave content to the notion of God the Father as confessed in the first article of the Creed. When the three Persons of the Trinity were seen as perfectly open to the other and inter-dependent, mutually indwelling each other, living in one another by virtue of eternal love (John 17:21), then the monarchical and patriarchal picture of God the Father as Head of a divine household gave way to a picture of fatherhood based on. *love* and not lordship, on mutuality and not domination, on common life and not subordination.

11. Confession of belief in God the Father thus affirmed a *network of re-lationships*: God is Father of the Son within the Trinity, Father of the Son incarnate as Jesus Christ and Father of all who by the power of the Holy Spirit are incorporated into Christ, become adopted sons and daughters of the one Father, and are thus enabled to confess God as truly "Our Father". The sense of Father in each of these several relationships must be differentiated. God cannot be called Father of creation in the same sense as he is called Father of the Son, or Father of all who are joined with the Son. But all of these senses cohere in Christ and are grounded in the eternal Trinity.

III. THE BIBLICAL WITNESS

12. Although the Father–Son image is used in the *Old Testament* to describe the relation between Yahweh and the people of Israel, it is only one amongst many images. What is however most striking is the character of God's fatherhood that is stressed. The *Lord* is Israel's father because he "bought her with a price" (Deut. 32:6). The reference is to the deliverance from Egypt, the act of creation and redemption which brought the nation into being. "When Israel was a child I loved him . . . out of Egypt I called my Son . . . I led them with cords of compassion" (Hosea 11:1,4). In two passages in Jeremiah, God's fatherhood is seen in his caring, comforting and nurturing his young child (Jer. 31:9; 3:4). In Isaiah,

fatherhood is closely connected with God's compassion upon his son and the word Father is used in parallel to Redeemer (Isa. 63:16; 64:8).

13. Clearly what stands out is neither the maleness of God, nor a patriarchal picture of a repressive authoritarian father. Rather, the qualities associated with God's fatherhood are those which have been designated as feminine and quite wrongly assigned only to women. The Old Testament picture of father might more accurately be described as that of a *motherly father*. This is further supported by the motherhood images used of God. Yahweh is likened to a protective mother bird (Isa. 31:5); a midwife (Ps. 22:9); the mother conceiving (Num. 11:12); the pregnant mother (Isa. 46:3); the mother giving birth (Isa. 66:13); the suckling mother (Isa. 49:45); the mother comforting her child (Isa. 66:13). Although these powerful images of motherhood are used of Yahweh, Yahweh is never addressed as "Mother" as God is addressed as Father.

14. In contrast to the Old Testament the notion of the fatherhood of God is central in the *New Testament*. Again and again Jesus uses the term *Abba* to address his Father. The unprecedented use of the term Abba for God evokes a close, familiar relationship. Although by the time of Jesus the word was used by adults, it was more often addressed by children to their father. Jesus' relationship as Son to God the Father echoes throughout the gospel stories. At the beginning of his life, the story of the Virgin birth in Matthew and Luke points to the way in which God is "uniquely his Father". And at the end of his life in Gethsemane Jesus cries "Abba, Father" (Mark 14:36) and, finally, on the cross he commends himself into his Father's hands (Luke 23:46). So close is the relationship between Jesus and his Father that he could say to Philip: "he that hath seen me hath seen the Father" (John 14:9).

15. It is not only Jesus who calls God "Abba", for he commands and permits his disciples to address God as "Abba", *"Our Father"*. St Paul indicates that God is our Father because he is first the Father of Jesus, who graciously allows us to share in that unique Father–Son relationship. It is the Spirit who unites us with the Son and who sets us free as his brothers and sisters by adoption, to call God "Abba". What Paul says of "sons" he says also of daughters (2 Cor. 6:16–18): communion with the father is open to all human beings without differentiation. "For as many are led by the Spirit of God, these are sons of God. For ye received not the Spirit of bondage again unto fear; but ye received the Spirit of adoption whereby we cry Abba, Father" (Rom. 8:14–15). "And because we are sons, God sent forth the Spirit of his Son into our hearts, crying Abba, Father" (Gal. 4:6). As individuals and as the church we call God Father in, with and through Jesus Christ, as adopted sons and daughters.

IV. TODAY

16. The various meanings contained in the credal confession of God as Father each carries a rich connotation for Christians today. The confession of God as *Father of all human beings* implies that Christians are called to live in a familial relationship with all peoples. This demands an awareness of others and an openness to them. Moreover, God as Father of all gives gifts to all his children, not only to Christians. The givenness of the familial relationship demands that the inter-relatedness of the human family is taken seriously. What is done in one part of the world has profound consequences for, and repercussions upon, other parts of the human family. Christians are asked to share with and care for all who are their brothers and sisters in their joys and sufferings.

17. But Christians are also part of the inner *family of God*, made sons and daughters through their incorporation into the Son, Jesus Christ. They are to recognize the way their Father nurtures and cares for his children, and nowhere more truly than in the gift of himself in the eucharist. In the eucharist Christians focus their brothers and sisters in their joys and sufferings.

18. Just as the Father of Israel and the Father of Jesus Christ required obedience, so Christians are called to a life of obedience. God the Father is not the coercive, authoritarian, domineering Father who holds his children to him by force. He stands back, allows his children space and freedom to become what he wills them to be. Just as when Israel was unfaithful God disciplined his children so Christians are disciplined in love and mercy as they grow, through the power of the Spirit, into the *full stature of sons and daughters* of their heavenly Father. But, as the Son's obedience to his Father drew him along the road of suffering and obedience even to death, so Christians are called to follow that same way, knowing that as in his fatherly love God raised his Son from death, and that in the same love the Father wills to give to all his children the gift of eternal life.

19. In calling God Father neither the Bible nor the Creed intended to assign to God male gender or biological fatherhood nor only the one-sided qualities we have defined as masculine and assigned only to men. We discover a *fatherhood* which embraces and transcends human differentiations and the limitations of role and gender. While not wishing to surrender the confession of faith in God the Father, nor the address given by Jesus to his disciples, "Our Father", we recognize a need to uncover the silent but complementary part of the tradition of a feminine face of God. Further we believe that Christians are free to explore language, symbols and imagery which celebrate the feminine in God. It is this God who encompasses and transcends male and female, masculine and feminine, who liberates both men and women from the false stereotypes of masculine and feminine which have entrapped us all.

20. As we learn to celebrate the *"motherly Father"* we revalue the feminine in human life and are offered new possibilities for achieving integration within each person as well as complementarity between women and men. The "motherly Father" is moreover the God who cares for and nurtures all his children, the one concerned for the weak, oppressed and the most vulnerable, the children. And it is this God who loves and shares all that he has, who judges hierarchical structures when they oppress and dominate in the church and in the world. To confess God as Father is to acknowledge a wholeness in God which we are called to reflect in ourselves, in our relationships with each other, in the life and structures of our society and not least in a renewed community of women and men in the church.

> *Commentary:* While we all agree both that we must continue to confess our belief in "God the Father Almighty" as a given part of our Tradition and also that we need to recover a feminine face to God, there is as yet no agreement amongst us as to whether we may go on to address God as "Our Mother". However, the fact that saints and mystics in the past have felt free to address God both as Father and Mother gives many the confidence to use both forms of address in their prayer to God.
>
> "As truly as God is our Father, so just as truly is he our Mother" (Julian of Norwich).

b) The Almighty

21. The almightiness of God has often been understood and presented as sheer, absolute omnipotence, naked, irresistible power, the capacity to do whatever one wants. Such omnipotence seems to exclude the possibility of genuine freedom for any of his creatures; it can also pose the question, in the face of evil, sin, injustice, suffering and death, whether an omnipotent God can possibly also be good and loving. As an ancient dilemma puts it: "As the world is manifestly imperfect, its creator cannot be both good and all-powerful, for if he were both, the world for which he is responsible would be perfect. If he is omnipotent, he cannot be good; if he is good, he cannot be all-powerful." The affirmation that the Father is almighty thus seems to face us with an unresolvable problem of theodicy. But is the idea of omnipotence presupposed here the same as what the Creed affirms? The Creed itself suggests not.

II. THE CREED

22. The Greek term used here in the Creed is *Pantokrator*, literally, "the one who holds and governs all things". It does not mean, in an abstract way, "one who can do anything he wants", but rather "one in whose hands all things are". It is less a description of absolute omnipotence than of universal providence. To call the Father *Pantokrator* is to affirm that the whole universe is in his grasp, that he does not and will not let it go.

23. At the time of the framing of the Ecumenical Creed in the fourth century, the wording and content of the first article were not controversial (though its relation to the second and third articles and their connection with it formed the pivot of the entire debate with Arianism). Its elements were already well-established common ground, solidly anchored in the tradition of faith, worship and theology. That tradition, however, had to be maintained and defended in earlier *conflicts with Gnosticism*, which drew a radical distinction between the Father of Jesus Christ and the Creator or cause of this material universe. The identification one God = Father = Pantokrator = Maker of heaven and earth was successfully upheld in the face of the determined opposition from those who could not and would not accept the goodness of creation or the Creator, who could not and would not believe in a Creator who was also Redeemer, who could not and would not recognize that the God of Israel was the Father of Jesus Christ, that the universe was indeed guided and directed by his sovereign providence. It is in this setting that the particular force of the inclusion of *Pantokrator* in the Creed is to be understood.

24. At the same time, the affirmation that the Father is also *Pantokrator* brought with it (at least in principle) the dethroning of all other claimants to universal sovereignty, to government and mastery over the world and its history and destiny. There were many such *claimants*: the Hellenistic pantheon; deterministic Fate; the Platonic Forms; Aristotle's Unmoved Mover; the impersonal World-Reason of the Stoic philosophy; the esoteric teachings and rituals of the mystery religions; the Gnostic archons; or even — not least! — the apotheosis of earthly dominion in the Roman imperial cult. Against all of these the church and the Creed affirmed: the Father of Jesus Christ, and none other, is *Pantokrator*.

III. THE BIBLICAL WITNESS

25. The *Old Testament* is full of testimonies to the power, majesty, sovereignty and faithfulness of God as displayed in creation (e.g. Ps. 93), in the ordering of the

natural world and — above all — in the history of Israel, most particularly in the Exodus from Egypt. But the Old Testament never speaks of an abstract omnipotence, but of God's power manifested in action. It was also only relatively late that it came to proclaim the God of Israel as Creator of the world and sovereign over all other powers. The circumstances of this proclamation are of significance. It came in the time of the Exile after the destruction of Jerusalem and the Temple, after the apparent humiliation and defeat of Yahweh by Marduk, the god of Babylon in the days when Israel's trust in him might seem to have lost all basis. It was precisely then that Deutero-Isaiah announced that this God ruled over the world and its history, that the gods of the nations were mere idols and their rulers instruments of his purposes, and, not least, that he remained faithful to his covenant. The message was one of promise, mercy and assurance in spite of all that appeared to contradict it in the existing state of affairs. Its ground lay in Yahweh's strength and faithfulness: "But now thus says the Lord, he that created you, O Jacob, and he that formed you, O Israel: Fear not, for I have redeemed you; I have called you by name, you are mine" (Isa. 43:1). Thus says the Lord, the King of Israel and his Redeemer, the Lord of hosts: "I am the First and I am the Last; besides me there is no god . . . Fear not, nor be afraid" (Isa. 44:6–8). His might is paradoxically revealed in and through the suffering of his servant (e.g. Isa. 49).

26. The use of the word *Pantokrator* in the *New Testament* is strikingly similar. It is a relatively rare word in Greek, but was used on a number of occasions in the Septuagint to translate Hebrew expressions whose original meaning is now obscure, but which are usually rendered as "Almighty" (El Shaddai) or "Lord of hosts" (Adonai Zeḅa'oth). In the New Testament it occurs only a few times, all but one in the Apocalypse. Characteristic is Revelation 1:8: "I am the Alpha and the Omega, says the Lord God, who is and who was and who is to come, the *Pantokrator.*" The *Pantokrator* is the First and the Last, he who was and is and will be. As such, he is God and Lord. The affirmation has both a clear liturgical ring and an apocalyptic colour. It is a solemn, longing and jubilant cry of praise and hope in the midst of a dark and profoundly ambiguous world, a world indeed which appears to be in the hands of Antichrist. The same note of confident trust is struck in the single New Testament passage outside the Apocalypse in which *Pantokrator* is used — 2 Corinthians 6:16–18. This hymns the faithfulness and the calling of God (with rich echoes of Old Testament prophecy) and ends: "and I will be a father to you, and you shall be my sons and daughters, says the Lord *Pantokrator*" (v.18). This points us to the authentic sense of the affirmation of the Father as *Pantokrator* in the New Testament itself: it is doxological and eschatological, testifying to the faithfulness and ultimate sovereignty of God as the ground of faith, confidence and trust — and also of our calling and obedience.

27. The affirmation has, however, a yet deeper ground in the gospel, and one which more than all that has been mentioned so far discloses the nature and quality of God's sovereign power. For that power is not simply a projection, magnified to the nth degree, of worldly authority and imperial pretensions. Nor is it simply a kind of universal cosmic energy or an irresistible force of history. It is a freedom and a sovereignty so transcendent that God could enter into his own creation in the incarnation, and there victoriously assert his claim upon it in and through what appeared to be the absolute and final negation of his power, the crucifixion of the incarnate Son. It is not enough to regard the cross as a kind of temporary eclipse of God's sovereign power, subsequently followed by its triumphant vindication in the Resurrection. In the apparent defeat, in the *powerlessness of the cross* and the death

of the Crucified lies the assertion and realization of God's sovereignty and providence over and in a world estranged from him. God did not let go of his creation, but in the Son assumed human nature and held fast to it into the jaws of destruction. Only supreme freedom, love and power could so express itself and maintain its hold through death to resurrection. The crucified Christ is "the power of God and the wisdom of God. For the foolishness of God is wiser than men, and the weakness of God is stronger than men" (1 Cor. 1:24–25). This is the sense in which God is supremely *Pantokrator*, the one who holds all things, in whose hands the world and its destiny are securely grasped *in spite of* the reality of evil, sin, suffering, and death.

To return to the Creed: the full depth of the first article is only disclosed in the second, for it is there that the inner quality and character of the divine sovereignty and providence are spelt out in Jesus Christ as those of a love which claims, holds fast, redeems and restores, and which is stronger even than death. Here is revealed the profoundest *intensity* of the divine lordship which in its full *extension* stretches out to include the whole created universe and in its intention drives towards the reign of God in the new heaven and new earth.

IV. TODAY

28. The affirmation of the *Almightiness* of the Father in the sense intended by the Creed remains as relevant today as ever before, indeed bears directly on urgent questions and concerns of the present time. The confession itself has not changed; it is the same yesterday, today and tomorrow, as is the One whom it recognizes, celebrates and proclaims. But the challenges to faith today mean that it could be both appropriate and fruitful for our common confession to recover and articulate afresh the sense, simply yet powerfully expressed and conveyed in the Creed, of God's sovereignty over, in and for the world he has made of which we are part.

29. First, the affirmation today is, as in every previous age, one of *faith*—faith that God will carry through his gracious and merciful purposes for humanity and for the world to their consummation and realization through the establishing of his kingdom in a new heaven and a new earth. Faith learns from that anticipation to distinguish between what is still hidden, but will be, and what is now, but will not endure. In particular, it draws from it the confident assurance that "the powers of the present age"—whether political, economic, scientific, industrial, military, ideological or indeed religious—do not control and will not have the last word concerning the destiny of the world and humankind. The Lordship of the Almighty relativizes and judges them all. The confession of faith in that Lordship, that Almightiness, is itself subversive of all other claims to sovereignty, a challenge to every form of enslaving bondage, a celebration of the liberating strength of the Creator of heaven and earth, and a sign and testimony of hope for each individual and for the whole created universe. The church is called to affirm and proclaim this faith against all appearances to the contrary, not only as its own deep longing, but as the promise and word of the Lord.

30. Second, this proclamation and commission is one of *hope* in the face of all that now ominously threatens the future of the world and the human race: the nuclear arms-race between the super-powers with the apocalyptic nightmares it generates; the ecological crisis; the catastrophic imbalance in the distribution of material resources and their economic exploitation between different countries and regions of the world; the appalling reality of violent conflict, senseless war, inhuman tyranny, oppression, injustice and persecution. Whatever the future may

bring, whatever evil may be inflicted or suffered, none can fall out of God's hand. This hope gives confidence to witness to the sovereignty of God in word and in action, to resist the forces of destruction, to recognize and proclaim that he is Lord of all areas of life, both individual and societal.

31. Third, the character of God's sovereignty as other-affirming and self-giving love evokes and enables *love* for God and neighbour as the motive and dynamic of Christian life and service. The Almightiness affirmed in the Creed is that of *the Father* who so loved the world that he gave his Son. The church needs constantly to be on guard against presenting him as if he were a tyrannical despot; against the temptation to approve or support authoritarian oppression in his name; against understanding and projecting its own mission and calling as an exercise of power and control over its members or society at large. The gospel proclaims the Almightiness of the Father as the reality of eternal love, strong to create, maintain and redeem the children of God, and liberating them to grateful service in that same strength, the love of God poured out in their hearts by his Spirit.

c) Conclusion: the Father Almighty

32. Implicit in all that is said above is that "Father" and "Almighty" *mutually* qualify each other. It is the Father, and no other, who is the Almighty; and as the Father he is indeed Almighty, and nothing less. To speak only of the Father, forgetting that he is Almighty, risks trivializing and sentimentalizing the divine fatherhood; to speak only of the Almighty, as if he were not also Father, is to risk projecting a demonic vision of sheer arbitrary power as if that corresponded to the reality of God. Only when the two aspects are both seen together, and their interpretation controlled by the revelation of their meaning in Jesus Christ, are these dangers guarded against.

33. The Father is indeed *almighty*. He is not powerless to achieve what he will, to fulfill and complete his good purpose for humankind and the whole creation. His power transcends all other powers which are created by him and remain subject to him. As such, it is a power of a radically different order and quality from them all.

34. The Almighty is indeed *Father*. He is not an indifferent or uncaring ruler who seeks only to exploit and dominate his creatures. His love establishes them in relative freedom and independence, allowing them even to revolt against him and reject him. Yet even there he accompanies, supports and reaches out to redeem them as, we may say, the "motherly Father".

35. The *Father* is not the God projected by deism, absent from and unaffected by his creation. Nor is he the God of theism who engages with the world only "from above". Nor is he merely creative power or absolute will as proclaimed in some religions and philosophies. In dialogue with such views the church should not too quickly assume that the first article of the Creed is common ground with them, for if the decisively Christian element is missing the entire perspective is altered. The One God affirmed in the Creed is not only Maker of heaven and earth; he is the God of Abraham, Isaac and Jacob, the God of the Exodus and the covenant, above all the good Father of Jesus Christ — and as such also the *Almighty*.

C. THE CREATOR AND HIS CREATION

I. THE THEME

1. Together with people of other faiths, e.g. in Africa, Christians believe that the world in which they live is not an autonomous entity, having its origins, life and destiny in itself. Rather they believe that the world and the whole cosmos, things seen and unseen, are the work of a *Creator* God, who is not only the cause of its being but also the continuing source of its life and final goal of its existence.

2. This belief in a Creator God and a created cosmos is *confessed* in the first article of the Nicene Creed on the basis of the biblical witness which gives the Christian belief its specific content over against that of other religions. How then is this fundamental Christian confession of a Creator and a creation and the relation between the two to be interpreted?

3. Christians confess a *Trinitarian God* in relation to the world as creation. God the Father created the world from nothing through his word. God the Son became part of creation in the incarnation. God the Holy Spirit is continuously active in the creation leading it to its final consummation. What are the implications of this comprehensive Trinitarian perspective, e.g. for the relation between creation and redemption?

4. The concern for the "integrity of creation" (Vancouver 1983), for the preservation, responsible use and just distribution of the resources of this world and the survival of the whole world and of humanity in face of the nuclear threat has become an issue of life or death in our times. What are then *basic orientations* which can be developed on the foundation of the Christian confession of God the Creator and of the world as his creation for a Christian contribution to the common human concern for the integrity of creation?

II. THE CREED

5. The church inherited the Old Testament faith that God is "the Maker of heaven and earth, the visible and invisible world" (Gen. 1; cf. Col. 1:15f.), and like ancient Israel, it had to face questions about the goodness of God's creation and of the mystery of evil in the world. In the first centuries after Christ the interpretation of creation became again controversial when heretical teachings drove a sharp wedge between the visible and the invisible world, between matter and spirit, the God of the Old Testament and of creation on the one hand and the God and Father of Jesus Christ on the other, between Israel and the church, between the Old Testament writings and the New Testament scriptures. At the time when the Creed was formulated at the Council of the fourth century, it was necessary to reaffirm the faith that God the Father is also the *Creator*, in order to exclude heresies which denied the identity of the creator and the God and Father of our Lord Jesus Christ (e.g. Marcionism and Gnosticism). Faith in the creation of all there is as God's handiwork once again affirmed the created world as the good work of God the Father and, at the same time, of the Son "through whom", as the second article confesses, "all things were made", and not an evil world hostile to God. God is the Creator who created a good world and also a good humanity. He is not just the one who redeems humanity *out* of the world and *from* the world.

6. God made not only the *heavens* but also the *earth*, not only the visible but also the invisible world. The visible world, too, is good and not evil; it comes from God and not from the devil. In its struggle for a proper understanding of the world and humanity's existence in it, the church thus emerged not with a world-denying,

but with a world-affirming faith. Likewise, the invisible intermediate world, the "metaphysical" realm, the "things between heaven and earth", the numinous forces — all that which the ancient world worshipped as divine — is not divine but belongs to the world created by the one true God. Even the invisible and spiritual things, the subconscious and suprasensible realities, are part of the created universe. God the Creator alone is divine; the invisible world too, even the heavens, are his handiwork.

III. THE BIBLICAL WITNESS

7. *Israel's* creation faith which has found its classical expression in the well-known creation stories of Genesis 1–2, owes much to the religious traditions of the ancient peoples of the Near East, the Assyrians, Babylonians, and the Canaanites. However, what Israel has received, it has also drastically transformed and re-moulded to express its own response to God's revelation. The dualistic myths and theories of the origin of the world which were known among Israel's neighbours assumed a pre-existent matter or partner or opponent outside God which is party to the event of creation. By contrast, Israel confessed that there is nothing besides God that is not "made" and does not owe its existence to him. The *whole* creation — the heavens as well as the earth, the visible and also the invisible world — has come into being through God and is completely dependent upon him as its Maker (Gen. 1–2; Ps. 8; Isa. 44:24; Matt. 5:34–35; Acts 4:24; 14:15; 17:24; Eph. 3:9; Rev. 4:11). Thus distinguishing clearly between the Creator and the creation, Israel has drastically demythologized the ancient understanding of all reality.

8. The confession of God the Maker of heaven and earth rings full of praise, for creation bears witness to *God's incomparable majesty* which he shares with no other (2 Kings 19:15–19; Neh. 9:6; Isa. 40:25–26); it shows forth God's wisdom and power (Ps. 104:24; Prov. 3:19–20; Jer. 10:12–13; Rom. 1:20–21); it bears witness to God's steadfast love and care (Ps. 136:4–9; Matt. 6:26–32). The majesty of God, reflected in his works of creation, is the basis for worshipping and thanksgiving for trusting and obeying him (Ps. 95; Isa. 40:27–31). God stands in a *personal, covenantal* (Gen. 8:22; Jer. 33:20) *relationship to his creation*: his divine decree determines its order (Gen. 1:14–19; Job 38:33; Ps. 104:9; 148:6; Jer. 5:24; 31:35–36), and his continuing power upholds and renews the creatures (Ps. 104:29–30). It is at God's command that the earth produces vegetation and animals (Gen. 1:11–12, 24–25). Through his word God directs the course of history and shapes the lives of women and men (Jer. 1:9–10; Isa. 55:10–11; Heb. 4:12). All creation, including inanimate nature, is praising its Creator (Ps. 148).

9. In the *New Testament* the soteriological and eschatological significance of creation, already broached in the Old Testament, comes to the fore and is reflected upon in the context of the work of Jesus Christ and of the Holy Spirit: God the Creator is the First, and he is also the Last (Isa. 44:6; 48:12). He created in the beginning, he creates now, and he will create in the future (Rev. 1:4, 8; 4:8). In the end God will be all in all (1 Cor. 15:28) and there will be "a new heaven and a new earth" (2 Pet. 3:13; Rev. 21:1; cf. Isa. 66:22). Creative renewal through God's Spirit is experienced by God's people (Ez. 36:26–28; Jer. 31:31–34) who in Christ — the agent of God's creation (1 Cor. 8:8; Col. 1:17) — become signs of the new creation (2 Cor. 5:17; Gal. 6:15). But not only this, non-human creatures as well and nature itself will be transformed and will participate in God's new world (Rom. 8:19–23; cf. Isa. 11:6–9; 41:17–20; 43:18–21; Hos. 2:18).

New Testament writers see the design of creation in Jesus Christ (1 Cor. 8:6; John 1:1–18). God creates, sustains, redeems, and perfects his creation through Christ who is the centre of all there is (Col. 1:15–17; Eph. 1:9–10; Heb. 1:2–3). Living under Christ as its head (Col. 1:18; Eph. 1:22–23) and its members being continuously transformed into the image of God's Son (Rom. 8:29; 1 Cor. 15:49; 2 Cor. 3:18; 2 Cor. 4:4; Col. 1:15; 3:10), *the church* has a new and deepened vision of the sovereign purpose of the Creator and Redeemer whom to serve it has been called, firmly believing in the future resurrection of the body and in the life of the world to come.

Belief in the creative power of God's word (Gen. 1; John 1:1–3; Heb. 11:3) and the confidence that God is able to create "out of nothing" (Rom. 4:17; Heb. 11:3; cf. Matt. 3:9) are as characteristic of the Christian faith in God the Creator as is the conviction that everything has a beginning, that creation is the starting point of history, that all human existence has a historical character (1 Cor. 15:42–50; 1 Tim. 6:16) and that creation serves a divine purpose.

IV. TODAY

10. "The first article of the Creed suggests that the doctrine of creation should remain simply implicit." This was a conclusion of the Princeton consultation in 1981 on the doctrinal implications of BEM[1] and in Lima in 1982 it was stated: "The notion of God as Creator needs further work."[2] We agree that the *explication* of the first article is a timely and urgent task.

a) The Triune God as the Creator

11. The relative independence of the first article of the Creed implies that it is possible and meaningful to speak about God the Creator without first speaking about God the Son or God the Holy Spirit. It is here, in the first article, that the doctrine of *creation* has its original, primal and proper place. The one God, Father Almighty, is here confessed as "Maker of heaven and earth".

12. It is not possible to exhaust the meaning of the first article by referring to the second and third. It would be just as impossible to develop a Christian theology of creation *only* from the point of view of the first article. The *Trinitarian perspective* is indispensable from the beginning. The Triune God is the God who created all that is, the God *above* creation, the God before all time who through his word from the beginning created everything out of nothing, in Christ, "through whom everything is made", and in the Spirit, hovering over the waters. Already in and through the word of God, he entered *into* the creation. In the incarnation of the Son the Creator became himself part of the creation, the God *in* creation. The Spirit also is at work from the beginning as the creative giver of life. Thus the creation must be understood no longer in animistic or pantheistic terms but rather Christologically, incarnationally, spiritually and sacramentally — as the ongoing act of the Trinity.

b) The Creator acts — in redemption and revelation

13. While the first article deserves its own place, the ecumenical issue is not the doctrine of the Creator/creation *per se*. The question rather is how creation relates to revelation, redemption, sanctification, the new creation — all as acts of the same Triune God. That the Creed *begins* with the confession of the Creator has its theological significance also for the understanding of redemption and revelation.

14. In the faith of Israel God was the God of history who made himself known in decisive events. Israel knew, too, that this same God is the Lord of all history and of all other nations. But first of all Israel came to know him as the *God of the covenant* long before any clear understanding of God as Creator of heaven and earth was formulated.[3] It is important to recognize the theological relevance of the fact that the Creed first confesses faith in the Creator. At the same time it is God's saving act in the historical establishment of the covenant which is the revelatory presupposition for the biblical faith in creation. "The covenant is the internal basis of the creation, but the creation is the external basis of the covenant."[4]

15. God acts by his word, his word accompanies and interprets his acts. The Triune God "has not left himself without witness" (Acts 14:17), but revealed and continues to *reveal* himself in many and various ways in the world and in history. God reveals himself in his works, in creation, "in the things that have been made" (Rom. 1:20), and especially in the human beings who were created in his image and likeness, who "show that what the law requires is written in their hearts" (Rom. 2:15).

16. The knowledge of God given in his creation must not be isolated from the whole of the biblical revelation. Creation is a self-disclosure of God (Rom. 1:18); however, there is an essential difference between the incomplete knowledge of God attainable through creation and the self-disclosure of his mystery through the history of salvation which culminates in the event of Jesus Christ as a new unique and final disclosure. The *framework* of the unity of creation, nature, history and consummation is maintained, at the same time as this whole concept is deepened and elaborated through the experience of God's incomparable action in history in Jesus Christ.[5] It is in this wider perspective that the doctrine of creation has its proper place and significance.

c) God's good creation — and evil

17. God saw it was good — this is the chorus at every evening of the days of God's creation (Gen. 1). Also today it is important to Christian faith to emphasize the positive factors of life, the *goodness* of creation and its inherent possibilities for the future of humankind. Life is a gift of God. When God gave his mandates — already in the Garden of Eden, at Sinai, but also in the form of "the law written in their hearts" (Rom. 2:15) — it was to protect and promote life and the goodness of creation.

18. To believe in God the Creator is to begin to understand and to appreciate his creation. The more human beings come to recognize the marvels and the *dynamic* openness of the macrocosmos and the microcosmos, the more evident is the greatness and glory of the Creator. The Creator is still at work. The creation is going on around us and in and with us. This is existentially relevant here and now: "I believe that God has created *me* and all other creatures, that he has given *me* my body and soul . . . and still preserves them . . . " (Martin Luther). The creation is a dynamic reality, it is a *creatio continua*, going on towards its consummation.

19. But the goodness and wholeness of creation are constantly threatened by death and decay which are characteristic of the perishable life of the creation (cf. 1 Cor. 15:42ff.), and also by catastrophies in nature and the sufferings inflicted upon people by people. All nature and the whole of history are marked by that *ambiguity*, which is characteristic of this world as we know it in our daily experience. Relationships between God and his creatures are impaired — it was only the Creator himself who could recreate relations in Jesus Christ. The Creator

was the one who reconciled the world to himself (2 Cor. 5:19), and so affirmed the world as his creation and manifested his faithfulness to it. In him a new creation was revealed, a transformation started, beyond sin and brokenness.

20. The ambiguity and discontinuity are shown not only in man's rebellion against God, but in all creatures in all nature (Rom. 8:22f.). The whole creation is *waiting* for liberation. God's creative and redemptive work will not be complete until all powers of darkness are definitely brought under the rule of God as he wants the whole earth to be full of the glory of his covenant. The creation is from its origin pointing forwards, dynamically, eschatologically, to the day when Christ is to consummate the whole creation in the eternal kingdom of God.

d) Humanity in creation

21. The creation of men and women is described as the high point of the Creator's work. God also immediately employs the human beings as his cooperators and stewards (Gen. 1:26f.), even rulers (Ps. 8). He puts them *in charge* to take care of, use and develop his creation. Faith focuses not only on *my* Creator alone, but rather on the God who created everything, my environment, nature, the cosmos. And yet, the Creator gave special responsibility to all men and women in all times to be his representatives—to care for his "garden".

22. However, humanity has also refused to obey God's mandate, refused to be his representatives, and instead *abused* God's good creation. The freedom God had given was used, not to pursue his high calling, but to act contrary to God's will. Humankind, created in God's image (Gen. 1:27), turned away from God, and became the slaves of their own sin. And yet, he still holds an almost divine position (Ps. 8), even as sinner and in spite of his rebellion.

23. In Jesus Christ, as the firstborn of a new creation, God has *renewed* and continues to renew humanity. Women and men are continuously set free again to discover their Creator, released from the bonds of enslavement in order to be truly human, to live in "a new solidarity with all God's creatures".[6]

24. The first article emphasizes the creatureliness of all that is, and the humanness of our life in God's world. This has consequences for the whole Christian faith, including our understanding of the humanity of Christ, the view of the church as his body, the notion of the resurrection of the body—both Christ's and ours, the concept of sacraments with their use of *water, bread and wine*. In baptism we make use of water as a symbol of cleansing and renewal, and as part of the eucharistic celebration "thanksgiving is offered for creation as well as for redemption and sanctification" with bread and wine, "fruits of the earth and human labour", as "signs of the final renewal of creation".[7]

e) Consequences

(1) Humanity's mandate over nature and the destruction of our environment

25. The dominion over nature and creatures given to humanity (Gen. 1:26–28) and our special status as "image of God" (Gen. 1:27) as God's representative and steward above and over against creation, our nearly divine position, with nature "under our feet" (Ps. 8:6–7), are being made responsible for the exploitation of nature and the destruction of the environment. Blame is put at least upon the effect which these Old Testament thoughts have had due to their misunderstanding by man who has emancipated himself from God. Undoubtedly *the separation of the creation from the Creator* and the desacralization of nature through the Jewish and

Christian faith in God the Creator, together with the human drive for rational comprehension and an emancipating mastery over the world, have contributed to the origin and development of the sciences and technology — and thus also to the destructive results for our environment. Because of the transcendence of the Creator and his position *above* creation, in which man participates as God's deputy, man is not the brother of nature but its lord and master.

26. If the Old Testament is rightly understood, it does not legitimize by any means the exploitation of nature and the destruction of the environment. Quite the contrary, in his commission as God's deputy and *steward*, men and women are called to responsibility for God's creation, into which they remain embedded. Also according to Gen. 2:15 God's creation is a garden which man is told "to till and to keep". The creation belongs to the Creator, and as its steward the human person is accountable to God. The human being may use creation but must not exploit it.

27. However, an ethic of creation and environment, based solely on "stewardship", is in danger of being interpreted in an anthropocentric sense. According to such an understanding nature must serve human beings, it exists exclusively for their sake. Then the permission to eat meat (Gen. 9) can be misused as to lead to consequences like the millions of experiments made with animals today. People do not protect nature for its own sake, not because it is God's creation, but rather in order to protect themselves from the dreaded consequences of the destruction of the environment. Furthermore, modern science and technology have given us means and possibilities which go far beyond responsible "stewardship". An ethic, based merely upon the concept of human responsibility, does no longer suffice today when one considers the tremendous potential of science and technology and their impact upon nature, especially the threatening destruction of the world as we know it and the annihilation of humankind through atomic warfare. An anthropocentrically based ethic of the environment no longer suffices because the preservation of the creation demands of men and women the surrender of privileges and advantages which have been assumed because of their control over nature.

(2) Human responsibility in a world sanctified by the Triune God

28. It is possible to supplement an anthropocentric ethic of the environment with a creation-centred ethic, provided one does it from a Trinitarian point of departure. For God the Creator thrones *above* his creation; in Jesus Christ, however, he has entered *into* his creation, has himself become a suffering creature and is thus present *in* creation. The *Christological* basis provides faith in God's creation with the element of purpose and goal: the cosmos was created through Christ and to him, all things hold together in him (Col. 1:17f.). In Jesus Christ the Creator no longer simply stands over against or above his creation, rather he has himself become present in a world threatened by exploitation and destruction. A creation, into which the Creator has entered, is sanctified through the incarnation. Viewed Christologically, the Creator is not relegated to the past, rather he has presence and future: thus the *deistic* misunderstanding of the creation is avoided in that the *temporal* distance between the Creator and his present creation is overcome. And in Christ, the Creator is not only transcendent but also immanent; he is not only *above* the creation but also *in* creation: thus the *theistic* misunderstanding of the creation is avoided, namely the distance and the separation of the Creator from his creation which was expressed in the *spatial* symbol of the "beyond".

29. Furthermore, the preservation of God's creation is imperative also in light of the third article, i.e. from a *pneumatological* perspective. Also the "creation in

the spirit" links God's transcendence of the world with his immanence in it. As Holy Spirit God is present and at work creating and preserving life in the processes of the world. Through the Spirit God continues to give life and completes his work towards his new creation.

30. Creation is *sanctified* through the presence and activity of the Triune God in it. Whoever understands creation as sanctified through Christ and the Spirit, will also keep it holy, preserve and protect it. He/she will share the fruits of creation with justice; he/she will not arrogantly destroy God's creation and creatures by more and more sophisticated armaments, nor even use those to threaten them. Thus human responsibility for creation, which is commanded, is confirmed and supported inwardly as it were through faith in God, who has made the world in the beginning, who stands above it and who has entrusted man with dominion over it. The creation must not and cannot be destroyed through war or exploited ruthlessly because, through man as his co-builder, God rules *over* it, enters *into* it and continues to be at work in it.

31. All human responsibility in and for creation is exercised in the hope and assurance of the restoration of all creation.

NOTES

1. The potential contribution of "Baptism, Eucharist and Ministry" to the wider project "Towards the Common Expression of the Apostolic Faith Today", Princeton report, FO/81:9, November 1981, p.16.
2. "The Community Study and Apostolic Faith: Memorandum from the Working Group on the Community of Women and Men in the Church", in "Towards Visible Unity", Vol. II, M. Kinnamon ed., *Faith and Order Paper No. 113*, Geneva, WCC, 1982, p.48.
3. Cf. Bristol 1967, *Faith and Order Paper No. 50*, pp.9f.
4. Karl Barth, cf. *Church Dogmatics* III/1: The Doctrine of Creation, para. 41,2: Creation as the External Basis of the Covenant; para. 41,3: The Covenant as the Internal Basis of Creation; Edinburgh, 1958, pp.94ff., 228ff.
5. Cf. Bristol 1967, *op. cit.*, pp.11f.
6. Cf. "The Report from Montreal 1963", P. C. Rodger & L. Vischer eds, *Faith and Order Paper No. 42*, London, 1964, p.43.
7. Princeton report, *op. cit.*, pp.15f.

We Believe in One God, Father Almighty, Maker of Heaven and Earth

Aspects of an Ecumenical Approach
to the First Article of the Creed

DAN-ILIE CIOBOTEA

Introductory note

Introductory note

Of the ecumenical approach to the first article of the Creed, we have retained three major aspects: I. Faith in God and the challenge posed by atheism. II. The Christian faith in one God, Father, Son and Holy Spirit and the accusation of polytheism and idolatry. III. Faith in God the Father in the present age of feminist theology.

There are of course other important aspects, such as for example faith in God as Creator and human responsibility for the integrity of creation, but the limited space available obliges us to restrict our discussion to the three major aspects mentioned above.

In the following pages we shall give a brief presentation of the manner in which these three major aspects of the Christian faith have been the object of ecumenical reflection and effort on the occasion of the following meetings: (1) at Kinshasa (Zaire), March 1985; (2) Geneva, April 1985; (3) Crêt-Bérard (Switzerland), May-June 1985; (4) Stavanger (Norway), August 1985; and (5) Berlin/Potsdam (German Democratic Republic), July 1986.

I. Faith in God and the challenge·posed by atheism

The quest for visible unity of faith in a world marked by atheism, especially in Europe, is both difficult and necessary. True unity of faith cannot be achieved where there is no intensity of faith. For this reason the quest for Christian unity in the apostolic faith should be accompanied by a conscious realization on the part of the churches that they should make more effort, individually and collectively, to become confessing churches. Modern atheism, however, since it is born on "Christian soil" where it very often means the same as lapsing from Christianity, remains one of the greatest challenges facing the churches today, if not a judgment (*krisis*) upon them: a challenge which calls primarily not for apologetics, but for a humble and searching examination of the churches' contribution, past and present, to the phenomenon of atheism.

1. From the Kinshasa addresses

In the Kinshasa addresses the challenge of atheism was not discussed as an independent subject. *Sigurd Daecke*, the West German Lutheran theologian, did however tackle the modern challenges to the Christian creation belief in his paper on the "The Creator and his Creation". He sketched the constraints to which belief in creation and in God have both been subjected in the last two centuries. At the same time he identified some of the dimensions which must be opened up afresh if faith in God is to gain new credibility today.

> I *believe* — as the Nicene-Constantinopolitan Creed affirms in its opening words — in one God, the Father Almighty, Maker of heaven and earth, of all things visible and invisible. In other words, I *believe* in the Creator. Talk of the Creator is an utterance of belief; a confession of faith. "God the Creator", "God the Father", "Jesus Christ" as God's "Son" and our "Lord", and the "Holy Spirit" — these form a *single* series; occur in a *single* complex of specifically *Christian* doctrinal statements and items, of what must be *believed* and cannot be seen and known in the ordinary sense . . .
>
> In fact, however, the only reason why belief in God the Creator seemed simpler, easier and more self-evident than belief in Christ and in redemption, was because it had been reduced in the seventeenth and eighteenth centuries in a deistic direction to the simple statement of Gen 1 : 1 : "In (at) the beginning God created the heaven and the earth." Whereas Luther had already interpreted the doctrine of creation existentially by pointing to its significance for the individual (me) and his present life (my life now), this doctrine was now reduced to an affirmation concerning the past, about the beginning of all things, on which at that time science was still reduced to silence and could say *nothing*. The doctrine of creation was diminished to a doctrine of the origin of the world. In the first two chapters of Genesis, of course, this doctrine

still included a cosmogony—nowadays, too, this is often too little heeded—but this cosmogony was not the message and centre of the doctrine. Although the creation narratives of the Old Testament do indeed include affirmations concerning the origin of the world, these do not constitute the essence and distinctiveness of faith in God the Creator.

Reduced to a theistic doctrine of the origin of the world, however, belief in the Creator remained simple and easy and axiomatic only as long as science was unable to offer any plausible rival theory of the origin of the world on its own. The moment de Laplace was able to say to Napoleon: "I have no need of that hypothesis, Sire!" a far-reaching change began. The Creator God had been driven out of his first "gap". He thereby became "the god of the gaps", and one after the other the "gaps" were filled in by science, from the origin of the world down to the origin of life itself. The "automatic organization of matter" may still be disputed as to the details, yet even this last of the gaps, which the theologians still reserved for the Creator in the sense of "neo-vitalism" as recently as Karl Heim only thirty years ago, has finally been occupied by biochemistry—with whatever variations in detail.

Yet this very reduction of belief in the Creator to a doctrine of the origin of the world, to that with which this belief had only been combined, i.e. to the elements of a world-view from which it was possible and necessary to detach it, transformed the doctrine of the Creator, in the course of the nineteenth and twentieth centuries, from the simplest of doctrines into the most difficult and problematic, a doctrine which divided, not the confessions from one another, but certainly the church from the world. Belief in the Creator was the one doctrine which the modern world-view could least accept. Contradiction of faith in God the Creator reached its peak in the shape of Darwin's theory of evolution and, in particular, in the shape of the ideological absolutization of the doctrine of evolution in Germany by Ernst Haeckel at the turn of the century. Between the faith confessed by Christians and the modern scientific view of reality, belief in the world as God's handiwork ceased to be the area of greatest common ground and became instead the greatest factor of division . . .

About fifteen years or so ago, it became a matter of extreme urgency to speak once more not only of the Creator but also of his creation. For God's handiwork was being endangered and put in growing jeopardy by the exploitation of nature, by the pollution, contamination and destruction of the environment. It was inevitable that the doctrine of the Creator and his creation should move once more into the centre of witness and reflection. For the first time since it was first formulated sixteen centuries ago as an anti-Gnostic confession of faith, this doctrine is seen to be needed again today in all its richness, scope and complexity; no longer as something obvious and simple but as something challenging and difficult. Today, however, the issue is not so much whether the Creator in whom we believe is the Father of Jesus or on the contrary a demiurge. That is no longer the problem today. Nor is our problem today what it was a hundred or even just fifty years ago—namely whether there is any Creator God at all.

The issue today, rather, is *the world as God's creation*; the need to protect, preserve and rescue it. But it is possible to establish this obligation to protect, preserve and rescue the creation only if the environment to be protected and the natural world to be preserved can be confessed in faith as really *God's* handiwork. This, however, as we have seen, is precisely the question which the theology of creation has been the least concerned with in the last century and a half, when its attention has been focused primarily on God's word in Jesus Christ, on the human being as creature, and on human cooperation in the work of creation with a view to humanity's liberation.

These were and remain vitally important aspects of the doctrine of creation to which too little attention had previously been paid and which were discovered or rediscovered in the theology of our century. But too little attention was paid to the created world itself, along with God and Christ as Creator, along with the human being as creature and co-creator. This has to be made good today. Important contributions to making it good have been forthcoming in the past two decades from, above all, the American process theology associated with Alfred N. Whitehead, as well as from the Anglican sacramental theology of nature and evolution associated with William Temple. A first comprehensive and particularly outstanding contribution to this effort to find a new way of making God's handiwork, too, once again the theme of faith in the Creator has just appeared. Very significantly, the title of *Jürgen Moltmann's* recent "ecological doctrine of creation" is *"God in the creation"*. But first we must consider briefly the theme: the Creator *above* the creation.

2. The Kinshasa text

Even though, during the ecumenical session at Kinshasa, the problem posed by contemporary atheism to the Christian faith was not the subject of any in-depth reflection, its importance as a topic was underlined by the fact that it is mentioned in the first paragraph of the final text. This text states explicitly that atheism may manifest itself in many ways and that it could also be a challenge to believers to purify their notion of God.

> There are atheists in the sense of those who consider that belief in God, far from being the way of life and salvation, is rather a threat to the freedom and dignity of humankind; belief in God would rather be an illusion springing from psychological, sociological or economic grounds. In the early centuries, Christians were accused of atheism because they abandoned the pagan gods. Contemporary atheism may today be challenging believers to purify their notion of God.
>
> In face of the problems of existence in our world, some people are unable to find any transcendent or ultimate reference in life. Some of these place their hope for betterment in humankind itself. Others have abandoned the quest in a nihilistic way. (A.I, 1)

3. The subsequent revisions

a) To the discussion of atheism the revised text of *Geneva* contributes a few changes in externals only; not in the first paragraph, since that begins with the affirmation of the Christian faith in the one God, but in a commentary at the end of the second paragraph. This commentary accords a separate place to the statement in the Kinshasa text that the Christians of the first few centuries were accused of atheism because they had abandoned the heathen gods and refused to practise religious syncretism.

b) The revised text of *Crêt-Bérard* keeps the commentary on atheism of the preceding draft, but places it at the end of a different paragraph (No. 3), while the second paragraph is devoted mainly to doubt as opposed to the faith discussed in the first paragraph:

> Christians *believe* that "the One true God", who made himself known to Israel, has revealed himself supremely in the "One whom he has sent", namely Jesus Christ (John 17:3); that, in Christ, God has reconciled the world to himself (2 Cor. 5:19); and that, by his Holy Spirit, God brings new and eternal life to all who through Christ put their trust in him.
>
> Many people and religions other than Christianity profess faith in a single, universal god who is creator, redeemer and sustainer of everything. Others *doubt* whether there is any reality transcending the visible world, providing the source of its being and continuing life: for them a conception of God is no more than an expression and projection of human wishes and fears. Even when it is acknowledged that there are powers transcending the visible reality of the world the question is, can

it be maintained that there is only one such power and should that power be conceived as purely transcendent or also as immanent in the world and how can these aspects be reconciled? (I.A, 1 and 2)

However, what particularly distinguishes the revision made at Crêt-Bérard is the fact that reflections on the faith-atheism problem have been developed in two new paragraphs, 8 and 9. In this approach, the existence of God is presented as that which gives ultimate meaning to the whole of finite existence, and as the source of responsibility and hope in the world. Moreover, the text affirms that human nature is "inescapably religious":

> The world of finite things would lack ultimate meaning and purpose without the divine reality. Christians share with many other religions the belief that there is a God. Indeed, the very existence of anything finite remains an unresolved mystery without it. God is the source of obligation in a world where otherwise there would be no ultimately obliging reality as a criterion of individual behaviour. God is the source of hope in the face of perishableness, suffering, failure and strife, a hope surpassing everything that could be achieved by human efforts, but also inspiring efforts at creating a provisional state of order and human dignity.
>
> While the religious traditions of humankind are indeed all testimonies of human experience and thought, they support the fact that human nature is inescapably religious. Religions are not necessarily inventions of being whose primordial nature could adequately be described in purely secular terms as atheists assume. If the religious dimension belongs to the roots of the distinctively human predicament, then the fullness of being human is missed where the awareness of a reality transcending everything finite is obscured or extinguished rather than being attended to and sought after as source of possible answers and solutions to the promises, inadequacies and perversions of human life. (I.A, 8 and 9)

4. The Stavanger discussion

With respect to the problem posed by atheism to faith, the discussion group at Stavanger which analyzed and discussed the ecumenical work on the first article of the Creed was not satisfied with the treatment of the question of atheism in the commentary on paragraph 3 and in paragraphs 8 and 9. The same group recommended deeper study of the subject and even proposed the holding of a special consultation on it:

> The group feels that the treatment of atheism in paragraph 3 (Commentary) and in paragraphs 8 and 9 is not adequate. For one thing, atheism in the modern world assumes a variety of forms which require different types of response. The various forms of atheism are among the most serious challenges facing Christian faith today. We recommend that the challenge of atheism be mentioned in paragraph 2 and that there be a new section on "The Challenge of Atheism", probably after the present paragraph 15. We also suggest that the drafting of this new section be entrusted to a special consultation on the question of atheism.

In particular the Stavanger discussion group made the point that there is a need for clarification and deeper exploration of the statement that human nature is inescapably religious. "The statement that human nature is inescapably religious requires clarification. Is this true, either as an empirical or a theological statement? The question whether one can be truly human without being religious needs further exploration."

The Stavanger discussion group also recommended the introduction into the text of a special paragraph on *secularism*.

5. *The Berlin/Potsdam text*

This text stands out because of its exploration of the faith-atheism question, and takes into consideration the suggestions made at Stavanger. In paragraph 6 it is stated that faith in a creator God is confronted primarily by the "false gods" created by absolutized selfish human passions, and subsequently by doubt and denial of the existence of the one God. In paragraph 22, the Potsdam text returns to the description of the forms of contemporary atheism, and retains the affirmation of the previous texts that atheism also challenges believers to purify their notion of God.

Taking into account the criticisms formulated at Stavanger concerning the text's presentation of the relationship between faith in the one God and atheism, the Potsdam text, in paragraphs 24 and 25, contributed some clarifications.

Also worth mentioning here is the fact that the Berlin/Potsdam text devotes three new paragraphs to the problems of *idolatry* and *secularism* as phenomena opposed to faith in the true and sole Creator God.

These three paragraphs are important as an effort to explicate the importance and meaning that faith in the one God, Creator of heaven and earth, has today. Their content is as follows:

> So it can be seen that both in individuals and in groups the notorious temptation of *idolatry* is existing. It was for this reason that the Reformers spoke of the human heart as "forging idols". And the "production line" was not limited to the religious field. Of course, first and foremost "idolatry" is a category belonging to the phenomenology of religion. Nevertheless, and even in politics, one can everywhere experience the effects of the idolatrous tendency to absolutize a phenomenon or a power of nature, history or human civilization and to elevate it into an ultimate, or into something that gives direction and meaning to life. Everything in the world of humanity, be it destructive or creative, can in this way become an idol, a false god.
>
> This is a danger also in modern *secularism*. Of course the biblical inheritance contains a "demythologizing" element. A certain sober "secularization" is part of the historical task and contribution of Christianity. Hence there should be no preconceived rejection of developments towards secularization in culture and society such as have characterized the present age in Europe. However, the fact must not be overlooked that such trends themselves often became subject in a different way to the old temptation towards idolatry, with the absolutizing of their ideological, political or technocratic aims. A secularization which began as something quite legitimate has become an illegitimate "secularism".
>
> It is on the basis of the Creed and in the living confession of faith in God that the challenge of this secularism has to be faced. The warning of the prophetic and apostolic message against this tendency towards idolatry is persistent and emphatic: "You shall have no other gods before me" (Ex. 20:3f.). Thus the *faith in the one God* unmasks these gods as idols, illusions, destructive powers. It affirms and praises the one God, who alone — as Father, Son and Holy Spirit — is the giver of life in this world and the foundation of hope for the world to come. (I.A, 31–33)

It should nevertheless be made clear that the special consultation on atheism suggested at the time of the Stavanger meeting never took place; an ecumenical study of the problems posed by atheism to the Christian faith is therefore still necessary.

II. The Christian faith in one God, Father, Son and Holy Spirit and the accusation of polytheism and idolatry

Ecumenical meditation on the mystery of the unity of the church seems to be increasingly led in the direction of the mystery of unity in God, for no worldly model of unity can be the ultimate foundation of the unity of the church of God. On the other hand, the fact that many Orthodox churches, members of the WCC, have to an astonishing degree maintained and deepened their faith in the Trinitarian God under extremely difficult historical conditions and in frequently hostile environments can be explained by the fact that this faith represents the fundamental and irreducible dimensions of the Christian revelation, more precisely the revelation of God as Love. For these churches, the intensification of the dialogue with the other monotheist religions and with the scientific culture of our time should be achieved not "in spite of faith in the Trinitarian God" but with that faith as a starting-point. God's call to unity as manifested by the ecumenical movement is in effect a quiet but persistent call to a truer and deeper vision of unity.

1. From the Kinshasa addresses

As the session on the first article of the Creed took place in Africa, half of the papers were given by Africans. Two black theologians, Elonda Efefe from Zaïre and John A.K. Aniagwu, the Roman Catholic theologian from Nigeria, thus gave papers on Christian belief in God in the light of monotheism and polytheism. Aniagwu discussed in particular those challenges arising for the Christian, Trinitarian understanding of God as a result of the encounter with traditional religions and Islam in Africa:

> The African traditional conception of God must pose some *challenges* for the Christian faith in one God.
> "Diffused monotheism" is how one African scholar has labelled the African conception of God.[1] Perhaps for too long, foreign investigators were led into believing that Africans were polytheists, much like the ancient Greeks and Romans. The fact of the case, as the said scholar sees it, is that Africans are monotheists, polytheists and pantheists, all rolled up in one. They acknowledge one supreme God, who is lord and maker of all things in both the spiritual and physical domains. To that extent, they are monotheistic. But much of their cultic life is directed towards divinities and ancestors. Then they are polytheistic. Finally, the Africans recognize something of God (e.g. "vital force", "soul", "spirit", "fiat", etc.) residing in every single being in both the spiritual and physical domains. There, they would be pantheistic. Whence the use of the label "diffused monotheism" for their brand of belief in God . . .
> In the face of the current resurgence of African traditional religion within not a few patriotic circles, the challenge must arise for Christianity to justify its faith in a God who is both three and one, without being polytheistic or diffusely monotheistic like that of the traditional Africans.
> Also quite capable of generating some controversy is the Christian faith in a God who is provident, interacting directly with the world he created, as against the *deus remotus et incertus* of the Africans. What sense can it make to pray to God or worship him? Is it conceivable that his will can be influenced by anything man does or does not do?
> The fact should be acknowledged of certain congruencies between the Christian faith in God and the African traditional conception of him.
> To begin with, God's existence is accepted without question in either case. Whereas some Christians have been known to want to demonstrate or prove God's existence, Africans see that as a wholly unnecessary business.

As one African scholar says[2] there are no atheists in African society, such that an African (Ashanti) proverb can say: "No one shows a child the supreme Being". That is to say, everybody, including even the child, knows God's existence, almost by instinct.

In African traditional religion, as in Christianity, God is believed to be the creator of all that exists. But the notion of God creating the world *ex nihilo* does not seem to have found any place in the former as in the latter. All the known myths of the creation of the world in Africa portray God as having fashioned the world from pre-existing material. There is also the fact that the same myths often cast God's creative image as that of a moulder (Ila people) or carpenter (Tiv people). The traditional Africans, it would seem, did not go the further step to ask where the material God used in creation came from.

The idea of God being "personal" is not as explicit in African traditional religion as it is in Christianity. But certain attributes given to God in the former are suggestive of a belief in a personal God. For instance, God is portrayed as seeing, hearing, talking, thinking, feeling, sometimes even eating and drinking. All of these attributes, put together — especially thinking, feeling and talking — , suggest a person (or persons) behind them . . .

The radical, uncompromising monotheism of Islam is proverbial. In its view, "True faith (īmān) . . . consists of belief in the immaculate Divine Unity and Islam in one's submission to Divine Will".[3] Or else, as an Islamic scholar puts it: "The God of Islam does not reside in several divinities. He is absolute: the repository of all that is good and noble and sublime. Islam does not deny goodness and sublimity in others but it does not assign divinity to them because divinity, according to Islam, must be absolute and unadulterated with any human shortcomings or limitations. This amounts, as if it were, to the extraction of the qualities associated by some with divinity out of all divinities and vesting them in One Who transcends the limitations of others considered as divine."[4] Implicit in this statement is an unequivocal rejection of the Christian doctrines of the "Trinity" and the "incarnation" . . .

More often than not, the butt of their attack is precisely the Christian faith in a Triune God. A standard Muslim sermon or address would thus begin as follows: "Allah is one. He has no equal, no rival, no partner. He can have no son either, since he has no wife to bear him a son . . ."

In this connection, as a Christian, this writer believes that there is need for a re-examination of the Nicene formulation of the Trinitarian creed. One is here suggesting that, perhaps, the formula of *mia ousia, treis hypostaseis* does not convey the same meaning today as it did in the year 325 A.D. In our experience today, how much sense can it really make to claim that there are *three persons* in the *one nature* of God, when in every other situation that we know of, the reverse is the case: several natures joining to form one person (for instance, body, soul, spirit in the human person)?

It is probably this difficulty that has prompted a new way of looking at the notion of personality in God. According to this new approach, God would be said to be "personal", not one, two or three "persons". In other words, whatever God may be, he cannot be said to be person(s), since persons, in our experience, are essentially human. To say that God is three persons would thus give the impression of suggesting that he is three human persons. On the contrary, what is meant by saying that God is "personal" is that he is not less than persons; he has all the attributes of persons, and more. Whatever that "more" is, it is beyond the scope of human comprehension. All this is stated quite clearly in the following way by a philosopher of religion: "Most theologians speak of God as 'personal' rather than as a 'Person'. The latter phrase suggests the picture of a magnified human individual . . . The statement that God is personal is accordingly intended to signify that God is 'at least personal', that whatever God may be beyond our conceiving, he is not less than personal, not a mere It in relation to man, but always the higher and transcendent Thou."[5]

One wonders if this approach to understanding the notion of personality in God might not open new avenues for meaningful dialogue with Islam, especially if, as was said earlier on, both this latter and Christianity are willing to recognize the limitations in their formulations of the truth about God.

2. The Kinshasa text

First of all, the Kinshasa text makes the point that faith in the Trinitarian God has always been a stumbling-block for non-Christians and even in the church there are people today who feel the need for a new interpretation:

> For many people outside the Christian community, *the notion of the Triune God* has been a stumbling-block. Either it threatened monotheism as they conceived it; or, in the other direction, it excluded their own more multiple perceptions of the divine. Even within the church, many people today consider that the Christian doctrine of the Triune God stands in need of fresh interpretation and terminological revision. It may be that the work of clarifying the Christian doctrine of God both for those outside the church and for those within will best proceed hand in hand. (A.I, 3)

The Kinshasa text then explains how the Nicene Creed confesses faith in the one God, and defines the historical context in which it was formulated (A.II, 4–7). In paragraph 10, the Kinshasa text, under the heading "Today", explains that the one God of the Bible reveals himself in the history of salvation as an indivisible communion of life and love between three separate Persons: Father, Son and Holy Spirit. The text stresses that there is a profound link between the significance of the cross of Christ and the comprehension of the Trinity or of the one God who is Love.

Confronted by accusations from Islam of *polytheism*, or from Judaism of *idolatry*, Christianity must produce a response. The Kinshasa text states that whereas Jews, Muslims and Christians all in fact believe in one God, the revelation of God in Christ shows *how* God is one: not because he is an eternal "solitude", but because he is an eternal communion of life and love who reveals himself to human beings and calls them to share in him (A.IV, 14).

3. The subsequent revisions

a) The revised text of *Geneva* pronounces in favour of a more thorough-going dialogue with Islam and Judaism, and quotes the example of the apologists of the first centuries:

> In the early centuries, Christians were accused of atheism because they abandoned the pagan gods, and refused to practise religious syncretism. In this latter sense, Christians, believing in one God, seemed to stand apart from other religions. However, a closer look at the apologetic works of the early Christians shows that Christian theology was not totally opposed to the theologies of other religions but shared some common ground with them, especially with Judaism and religious hellenistic philosophy. This early Christian attitude, echoing St Peter's words in Acts 10:34f., is especially important today in view of the developing dialogue between Christianity and Judaism, or Christianity and other religions, especially Islam. (Commentary, I, A.2)

As for the Christian response to the accusations of Islam and Judaism, the Geneva text repeats with a few minor modifications the arguments of the Kinshasa text.

b) The revised text of *Crêt-Bérard* responds differently to the challenges posed by Judaism and Islam, but is chiefly distinguishable from the previous texts by its use of the idea of differentiated unity which holds together transcendence and immanence, a unity which does not exclude plurality. However, the arguments advanced by the Crêt-Bérard text, though more philosophical, mean the same thing as the previous texts, i.e. that in God unity is expressed in the indivisible communion of Three Persons:

The challenge posed by other monotheistic religions
Christians are sensitive to the fact that other monotheistic traditions do not share their faith in a Triune God. Christians, indeed, are often accused either of idolatry (Judaism) or polytheism (Islam). Although *Jewish* tradition knows of prophets who act on the authority of the God who sent them, Jewish faith considers it a violation of the oneness of God to associate any person with his eternal being. But Jewish tradition knows of realities that represent the transcendent God within this world — his name, his glory, his *shechinah*, and his *tora*. Do these realities which are distinguished from God's transcendent being really represent the presence of God himself? In that case the distinction between transcendence and immanence would also apply to the Jewish conception of the one God. On the other hand a transcendent God who could not be present in this world would hardly be the God of the Old Testament prophets. The Christian belief in the incarnation and in Jesus' eternal Sonship expressed in the Trinitarian Creed asserts the differentiated unity of God encompassing transcendence and immanence.
With regard to the *Islamic* charge of polytheism, it is important to stress that the Christian faith never intended to surrender the oneness of God. Nor did the Trinitarian doctrine of the church intend to limit or to weaken the affirmation of the unity of God. Rather, the Trinitarian differentiation of the unity of God is a condition of a truly consistent monotheism because it does not leave the principle of plurality outside that of unity so that unity would be a mere correlate to a plurality that were not included in the divine life. On the contrary, only the one God who has plurality within himself can be truly infinite and unlimited in his oneness. Only such a God can create a multitude of creatures who nevertheless, to some degree, remain united each within themselves as well as with others. (I, A.16 and 17)

4. The Stavanger discussion

During the Stavanger meeting, the participants requested that particular attention be paid to the relationship between Christianity and the other monotheistic religions, especially Judaism and Islam. At the same time, it was stated that one must recognize there is a great diversity of opinion on the question of the relationship between the various religions:

While we recognize why in the first article it is necessary to give special attention to relations with Judaism and Islam (mentioned in paragraphs 3,10,16,17) we wonder if it would be possible to consolidate this discussion.
There should be more recognition that there is considerable diversity in the way Christians approach the question of the relation between religions.

During the discussion it was also requested that in presenting the relationship of Christianity to the other monotheistic religions, a clear distinction should be drawn between Judaism and Islam, for it is from the Jews that Christians inherited their faith in the One God.

5. The Berlin/Potsdam text

The response to the challenges of Judaism and Islam does not greatly differ from that of the Crêt-Bérard text (I, A.27, 28). However the Potsdam text takes more specifically into consideration the challenge made to Christianity by other religions:

> In *other religions*, e.g., African traditional religions, Buddhism or Hinduism, the manifoldness of divinity is experienced in human beings and animals as well as in plants and things. They challenge the Christian Trinitarian belief as being too abstract and cut off from the realities of day-to-day life. Syncretistic movements such as transcendental meditation gain ground in Christian countries; they function often as compensation for the Christian Trinitarian faith which is no longer understood in its fullness, richness and concreteness. In face of these challenges Christians believe that the concreteness of the one God is no other than in the work of the Father, the Son and the Holy Spirit: the Father is the creator of every person, animal, plant or thing that exists; the Son reveals the meaning and healing of the Father's creation; and the Spirit brings divine life into every detail of heaven and earth. (I, A.29)

Present-day ecumenical thought is very positive in its insistence that unity in God is identical to the perfect and indivisible communion between the Father, Son and Holy Spirit. It is this unity — reciprocal communion of life and love — and not an arithmetical or abstract unity, that the faith of the church confesses and glorifies. And the fact that it is God the Father who is the source of this unity of communion shows that it is not a constraining, but a free unity. It is realized in the free gift of self between the Persons of the Trinity.

III. Faith in God the Father in the present age of feminist theology

Feminist theology is one of the important components of modern theological thought, especially in regions such as Western Europe and North America. Behind the disparate tendencies and uneven modes of expression manifested in contemporary feminist theology (or theologies), one can discern a genuine and legitimate aspiration towards a renewed and more authentic ecclesial koinonia based on the participation of all members and the recognition and exploitation of charismata which are frequently ignored. Because a patriarchal attitude and terminology have too often imbued the traditional Christian theology of all the churches, there is a current feminist reaction which goes so far as to query whether the designation God the Father may be in fact one manifestation of this patriarchalism. A constructive ecumenical study of this subject is necessary, in order to avoid the risk of over-hasty compressions and simplifications.

1. From the Kinshasa addresses

It comes as no surprise that at Kinshasa women had their say on questions raised by feminist theology about the traditional way in which God is confessed and understood. Mercy Oduyoye, the Nigerian Methodist, could not take part in the session herself, but let the participants have her contribution in writing. Its title is at the same time an outline of her programme: "We believe in one God: towards a non-patriarchalist understanding of God as Father".[6] In her contribution the vice-moderator of the Commission on Faith and Order, the Anglican Mary Tanner from London, spoke first about the fatherhood of God against an Old Testament background, before going on to deal with some feminist points of view:

> The Christian feminist challenges to the fatherhood of God have then to be seen as part of a much larger package, an interlocking agenda which touches our understanding of God, of women and men in God's image and the life and structures of the churches. To the question, is God really father, are the masculine attributes that

belong with fatherhood, power, lordship, kingship, mastery, any longer usable, not surprisingly feminists come up with different answers . . .

The majority of feminists, however, seek to overcome the patriarchal view of God in other ways. They cannot relinquish the concept of "God as Father" for it has been given to us in Jesus' own address to God and in his invitation to us to pray "Our Father". More than this through baptism we are incorporated into Christ, and are able to call God "Father" in, with and through Christ. Nevertheless, for Christian feminists it is vital to explode the myth that this fatherhood of God either takes its pattern from the pattern of human fatherhood as that has been perceived in any particular age or culture and also to explode the myth that to call God "Father" is to attribute to God maleness and biological fatherhood. The Kottayam report has already said it: "It is important to note when we speak of 'Father and Son' in their relationship to each other in the Trinity, we do not mean to imply that God is male. As a human being, Jesus Christ *is* male. But within the persons of the Trinity there is no gender." This may seem too naive an assertion to make in an explication of the creed today and yet many of the letters to the British press last year, when the Church of Scotland was debating the motherhood of God, revealed that in fact many do cling to the idea that God is male and that he exhibits primarily characteristics we have defined as masculine.

How then do feminists correct this one-sided view of God?

1. One way is to recover and lift up the silent, hidden part of the Christian Tradition, already there within the Old Testament and New Testament, and to find *a feminine face of God*. We have already referred to the Old Testament passages where a number of experiences which have been called feminine and wrongfully restricted to women are confidently used of God. Such thoughts continued in the church in Clement of Alexandria in the third century:

God is love
And for love of us has become a woman
The ineffable being of the Father has out of
compassion with us become Mother.
By loving the Father has become woman.

And it echoes most strongly in the beautiful writings of the mediaeval mystics. Mother Julian is one of the great discoveries of Christian feminists:

As truly as God is our Father, so just as truly
is he our Mother.
In our Father, God Almighty, we have our being;
in our merciful Mother we are remade and restored.

It is the uncovering of this silent tradition, hardly ever heard in the official worship of the churches, that restores a balance for women to a God with whom they have found it difficult to identify. This provides us with a courage to talk out of our experience about God and to form our words and our prayers. The tradition of a feminine face to God is there, silent, yes, but constant. It offers a rich corrective source.

2. But Christian feminists do not only ask the churches to complement the male-masculine language of God with female-feminine language. The most exciting development to me is that some feminist theologians, for example Rosemary Haughton, Patricia Wilson-Kastner, along with the Moltmanns are grappling with the content of God the Father and Jesus as Son and indeed with the doctrine of the Trinity. There is an attempt to "zero-content" *the notions of Father and Son*, so that they may be "filled out" again, not by a false patriarchy of the first century or seventh century or the Victorian era, nor even with our more enlightened twentieth century concepts of fatherhood, but filled out in faithfulness to God's revelation within the scriptures. If we concentrate on the notion of uniqueness in relation between Jesus and the Father, we see that the fatherhood of God, the Sonship of that Father, is so dramatically

different from that culture-bond tradition imposed upon them. The fatherhood of God is grasped most fully in relation to the centrality of the cross. The Father of Jesus is known as Father when he surrenders the Son to the cross. The Son knows what it is to be Son, when in complete obedience and conformity of will with the Father, he embraces the suffering of the cross. At the moment when Jesus surrendered in Gethsemane, and on the cross God gives proof of a radical difference from the all powerful, impassible God. At the moment when the Son suffers the abandonment of the Father, the Father suffers the abandoning of the Son, God gives up his pre-rogatives. Here the essence of fatherhood is quite other than what by comparison is seen as the poverty-stricken parody produced by patriarchy. This leads in the direction of what Moltmann and Rosemary Haughton call the "motherly Father": we begin to see that the title "God the Father" expresses a very different God from the God of much of the Christian past. It is precisely this God that many Christian feminists are searching for out of the depths of their experience as they reach out for the motherhood of God.

3. And finally, another important development for Christian feminism comes in *the understanding of the Trinity*. It is emerging clearly in feminist theology that the notion of the Trinity is far more supportive of feminist values. In *Western* tradition the Trinity has been viewed primarily in a monarchical way, with the Father as the source, the dominant one, who begot the Son eternally, and the Spirit proceeding from the Father (and the Son). God is Father and head of a divine household: his omnipotence, omniscience, absoluteness merely strengthened the patriarchal image. But in the *East*, the notion basic to the understanding of the Trinity is of God as relational. The three persons of the Trinity are part of what Moltmann calls "a social network"; the Trinity is "a social Trinity".[7] Each person is perfectly open to the other and interdependent. By virtue of their eternal love they live in one another to such an extent and dwell in one another to such an extent, they are one. This relational concept of the Trinity has a profound effect upon our understanding of the father-hood of God. The Trinity is based on love and not lordship, on mutuality and not domination, on common life and not hierarchy. This is very close indeed to the feminine perception of things. It "chimes" with women's experience, with their interest in equality, nurture and mutual support.

It is from this bringing together of experience with scripture and Tradition that the challenges of Christian feminism to the fatherhood of God spring. It is this which gives women confidence to write their own prayers and poems, even their own creeds. As one Roman Catholic nun says: "My secret worship of God the Mother has been the sure ground of my spirituality." This gives her confidence to write her own spiritual meditations:

We worship God our mother in solitude, seeking the secret places to be with her . . .
Everything in the garden magnifies her presence . . .
Everything pours from her source.
Everything participates in her being.
Everything is holy . . .
Searching for our Mother we run through trees,
lifting stones, kneeling at every pool and hollow,
looking into every cleft and beneath birds' wings.

Final reflections

1. The accusation that the church's language about God has been oppressively patriarchal needs to be taken seriously. Language functions within the community of faith. If some members find the language oppressive we cannot turn our backs on them. Religious language must nurture and sustain all of us.

2. We may not surrender the centrality of God the Father, Jesus the Son and the Holy and Undivided Trinity.

3. But we must understand the fatherhood of God through the unique relation of the Father to the Son, Jesus.

4. We need to recover the silent part of our tradition concerning the motherhood of God and the feminine face of God.

5. This will enable us to supplement the credal statement of belief in God the Father with images of the motherhood of God. At the level of necessary anthropology the masculine language about God should be balanced with feminine language, for God encompasses and transcends all that we understand by masculine and feminine.

6. My final reflection is in the form of a question. While not changing the words of the ancient creeds may we not also go on to address God as Mother: to say with Anselm, "Christ, my Mother, You gather your chicken with your wings" or with Julian of Norwich:

As truly as God is our Father,
so just as truly is he our Mother.
In our Father, God Almighty, we have our being;
in our merciful Mother we are remade and restored.
It is I, the strength and goodness of fatherhood.
It is I, the wisdom of motherhood.
It is I, the light and grace of holy love . . .
It is I who am the reward of all true desiring . . .

2. The Kinshasa text

The group who prepared the Kinshasa report thought deeply about the original meaning of the expression in the Creed "the Father Almighty", and arrived at the conclusion that this is the key expression for understanding the other articles of the Creed, and especially the fact that the confession of faith in "the one God" cannot refer to the Father in isolation, but to the Father in indivisible unity with the Son whom he begets and the Holy Spirit which proceeds from him. It is this Father, the source of the Trinitarian communion of eternal life, who is the Father Almighty, creator of heaven and earth (cf. B.I, 1 and 2).

The text next specifies the dangers implied in a faulty understanding of the expression "the Father Almighty". At the same time the group proposes to respond to certain challenges encountered by those who today confess faith in God the Father Almighty.

> The specifically Christian sense of the first article may be lost from view; one-sidedly authoritarian, paternalistic and triumphalistic associations may consciously or unconsciously colour its interpretation; these in turn may call forth protests and objections, issuing sometimes in rejection of the entire Christian faith. Such objections have indeed been directed against both "Father" and "Almighty" as suitable descriptions of God. They challenge us today to consider such questions as:
> — Can the fatherhood of God properly be understood in a non-patriarchal and non-authoritarian way?
> — Does "feminine" as well as "masculine" imagery have a necessary place in inclusive theological language? And, if so, can we go on to address God as "Our Mother" as well as "Our Father"?
> — In what sense do we affirm that God is the Father "Almighty"?
> — What is the relation or resemblance between the sovereign power of God and the "powers" at work in the world?
> — What are the similarities and differences between the Christian affirmation of the Father Almighty and comparable expressions used in other religions? (B.I, 3)

In its response to these challenges, the group first explains the *historical context* in which the Creed was formulated, or in other words the challenges which the fathers of the Council of Nicea had to face in their day (B.a.II, 4–7). The text then states that the eternal begetting of the Son by the Father is not identical with the biological father-son relationship in terms of the created human being. For this reason the eternal begetting of the Son by the Father confessed in the Creed was never meant to imply that the Father is male (B.a.II, 8).

The text insists on the fact that the true *fatherhood* of God is demonstrated in his relationship with his eternal Son become Man, given for the salvation of the world (John 3:16) (B.a.II, 9). A searching analysis of the description provided by the Gospels of the Father-Son relationship in the Holy Trinity shows that the divine fatherhood revealed in the New Testament has nothing to do with the image of a monarchical, authoritarian, power-hungry father.

As to whether God the Father may be considered also as a *Mother*, the Kinshasa group found first of all that the fatherhood of God in the Old Testament is shown in his love for the people of Israel, as their liberator and redeemer. On the other hand, there are in fact many expressions in the New Testament describing the relationship of God with his people in images of maternal affection. No-one, however, ever addresses the Lord as "Mother" (B.a.III, 12 and 13).

However, the group observes that the New Testament is distinguished from the Old Testament precisely in the revelation of God's fatherhood through his unique relationship with Jesus Christ, his eternal Son become Man (cf. B.a.III, 14). The extreme intimacy of the relationship of the Son of God become Man with his heavenly Father is expressed in the designation "Abba", and this intimacy constitutes the foundation upon which is for ever based that intimacy and familiarity which human beings who believe in the Son may have with the Father. Jesus' quality of being eternally the only Son of the Father is not communicated to other persons, but the intimacy of love involved in this quality is shared by the incarnate Son with all humanity and offered by him to all human beings who open themselves to him (B.a.III, 15).

On the basis of these findings, with the Bible and the Creed as starting-point and taking into consideration the present-day challenges mentioned above, the Kinshasa group concludes that *the true fatherhood of God* as shown in scripture and in the faith of the church cannot intrinsically be reduced to categories like masculinity or femininity.

Nevertheless, without wishing to "correct" the revelation and words of Christ, and without turning Tradition into something abstract or forgetting the disagreement within the group itself over the question whether one may address God as "Our Mother", the group thinks it necessary that in the description of the relationship of God with humanity there should be an attempt to "recover a feminine face of God":

> While not wishing to surrender the confession of faith in God the Father, nor the address given by Jesus to his disciples, "Our Father", we recognize a need to uncover the silent but complementary part of the tradition of a feminine face of God. Further we believe that Christians are free to explore language, symbols and imagery which celebrate the feminine in God. It is this God who encompasses and transcends male and female, masculine and feminine, who liberates both men and women from the false stereotypes of masculine and feminine which have entrapped us all. (B.a.IV, 19)

3. The subsequent revisions
a) The revised text of *Geneva* is chiefly distinguishable from that of Kinshasa for its combination of the two chapters "God the Father" and "the Almighty" of the Kinshasa text into a single chapter, "the Father Almighty". Here is an excerpt:

> The close association of Creator and *Almighty* with Father in the opening state-ment of the Creed tended to underline the idea that dominion and authority belong to the fatherhood of God. The Father God is the one who rules and wields authority over all creation, "the Almighty". The Greek term used here in the Creed is *Pantokrator*, literally, "the one who holds and governs all things". It does not mean, in an abstract way, "one who can do anything he wants", but rather "one in whose hands all things are". It is less a description of absolute omnipotence than of universal providence. To call the Father *Pantokrator* is to affirm that the whole universe is in his grasp, that he does not and will not let it go. At the same time, the affirmation that the Father is also *Pantokrator* brought with it (at least in principle) the de-throning of all other claimants to universal sovereignty, to government and mastery over the world and its history and destiny (I, B.4).

b) The revised text of *Crêt-Bérard* is to a great extent an abbreviation of the Geneva text. However, the Crêt-Bérard text puts more emphasis on the fact that in the language of Jesus (especially the writings of St John), "Father" is a name and not just an image or one designation among others.

The Crêt-Bérard text explains the image of the divine fatherhood in these terms, and retains in its final commentary the suggestion of "recovering a feminine face of God".

The image of fatherhood
When God is called the Father in the Bible, in Jesus' own teaching and in the Christian church, it was never intended to imply that God is male. Although the Trinitarian doctrine used the biological metaphor of begetting in its description of the eternal relationship between the Father and the Son, it is the relation of origin that is focused upon. In the biblical language God's fatherhood transcends the sexual distinction between male and female which had been part of the polytheistic concep-tions of gods and goddesses in Israel's cultural surroundings. God's fatherhood includes functions and attributes which belong to both men and women but which all too often in Western culture have been limited to women and called "feminine". In speaking of God the Father, the point of comparison is in the function of the father in the family, who cares for and nurtures all his children, the one who is concerned for the weak, the oppressed and the most vulnerable of his children. These parental functions include aspects of motherly care as well. God loves and shares all that he has, but he is also judging all attitudes and structures of oppression, domination and neglect in the church and in the world. To confess God as the Father is to acknowledge a wholeness in God which we are called to reflect in ourselves, in our relationships with each other, in the life and structures of our society and not least in a renewed community of women and men in the church.

"Father" as a name
In Jesus' language about God "Father" is not only an image, it is primarily the name of the God to whom he relates in his mission and whose kingdom he proclaims. It is the name used to address God in prayer. In its function as a name, the name of God in Jesus' own teaching and prayer, the word "Father" cannot be replaced by another one. It would no longer be the God of Jesus to whom we relate, if we would avoid the name Jesus himself used.

Commentary

While belief in "God the Father the Almighty" is a given part of the Christian tradition there is a need to recover a feminine face of God. However, there is no agreement as to whether God may also be addressed as "our Mother". In this discussion the distinction between image and name is important. While so-called "feminine" images illustrate the tenderness of God's love along with the image of fatherhood, it is a matter of Christian identity to continue to use the name that Jesus used in addressing God as he commanded his disciples to do. (I, B.32 and 33)

4. The Stavanger discussion

During the Stavanger meeting there were participants in the discussion group who took those who had prepared the previous texts to task for not having taken sufficient notice of the "Memorandum of the Working Group on the Community of Women and Men in the Church", drawn up at the session of the Faith and Order Commission, Lima 1982. This Memorandum had enquired:

How far are the terms Father, Son and Holy Ghost/Spirit, which safeguard the distinctiveness of persons, still adequate today to describe the Trinity? How far should the contention of many women that this language excludes them from the community of the body of Christ be taken seriously and lead us towards discussing new terms for confessing our belief in the Holy Trinity?[8]

On this subject the *rapporteur* of this discussion, Hans-Georg Link, justly remarked: "Without any doubt, a long process of interpretation still lies before us here. It is to be hoped that women will be more fully involved in this demanding and laborious work."[9]

5. The Berlin/Potsdam text

This text follows the broad lines of the previous texts both for the historical and biblical approach to the faith confessed in the Creed, and for the explication of the fatherhood of God and his omnipotence today. While trying to be responsive to certain challenges posed by modern feminist theology and to conserve in the text the recommendation of "recovering a feminine face of God", the group who prepared the Potsdam report stressed that the fact of addressing God by the designation "Father", as Jesus instructed his disciples to do, makes the Christian identity what it is (cf. I, B.48–50). Summarizing, the explication states:

In the first article of the Creed the identity of the one God is confessed first in terms of the *Father*. The one God is Father. To call God Father is the basis of all that is said about the one God. The Father is source of all divinity; the second article confesses further how this Father is the Father of the unique Son and finally the third article states that this Father is the one from whom the Holy Spirit proceeds. The fatherhood of God has to be understood in connection with the unique Son and the Holy Spirit. (I, B.47)

By way of conclusion, it may be said that ecumenical reflection on the apostolic faith is becoming today more and more essential, not only for the theological renewal of various churches but also for the dialogue Christians should hold with other religions.

However, a theological and spiritual deepening of the apostolic faith expressed by the Creed also contributes to a deeper understanding of what constitutes the church's true unity, which has its source and supreme model in the unity of communion of the Living God: the Holy Trinity.

In other words, common ecumenical reflection on the apostolic faith should help us to realize how profoundly the content of the truth of the faith is linked with what the material life of the churches and of each church member means at its deepest.

NOTES

1. E. Bolaji Idowu, *African Traditional Religion*, London, 1973, p.135.
2. John S. Mbiti, *African Traditional Religion*, London, 1975, p.29.
3. Art. "Islam", in *Encyclopedia Britannica* 9, 1980, p.912.
4. I.H. Qureshi, "Muslim Art", in *God and Man in Contemporary Islamic Thought*, Ch. Malik ed., Beirut, 1972, p.115.
5. John H. Hick, *Philosophy of Religion*, Englewood Cliffs, 1973², p.10.
6. Faith and Order mimeographed paper FO/85:16, March 1985.
7. Cf. *inter alia*, J. Moltmann, "Ich glaube an Gott den Vater. Patriarchalische oder nicht-patriarchalische Rede vor Gott?", *Ev. Theol.*, 43, 1983, pp. 397ff.
8. "Towards Visible Unity", Vol. II, M. Kinnamon ed., *Faith and Order Paper No. 113*, Geneva, WCC, 1982, p.48.
9. "Faith and Renewal. Commission on Faith and Order, Stavanger 1985", T. F. Best ed., *Faith and Order Paper No. 131*, Geneva, WCC, 1986, p.136.

PART II

The Second Article

We Believe in One Lord Jesus Christ

An Ecumenical Explication

Report of a Faith and Order Consultation
held at Kottayam, India, 14–22 November 1984*

A. Jesus Christ — True God and True Human Being

    I. The theme

   II. The Creed
     1. Of one being with the Father
     2. For our salvation he became incarnate
     3. Towards Christological convergence

  III. The biblical witness
     1. The Son of God
       a) The unique relationship between Jesus and his heavenly
         Father (Synoptics)
       b) The divine authority in the public ministry of Jesus (Synoptics)
       c) The eternal word of God (John)
       d) The self-giving love unto death (Paul)
       e) The stamp of God's very being (Hebrews)
     2. The humanity of Jesus of Nazareth
       a) Sharing in the human condition (Synoptics)
       b) The sending of the Son into the world (John)
       c) The other Adam (Paul)
       d) The learning of obedience through suffering (Hebrews)

  IV. Jesus Christ: True God and True Human Being for us today
     1. Contemporary experiences
       a) Concerning Jesus of Nazareth
       b) Concerning God
       c) Concerning our human being
     2. True God — for us today
       a) The God of Jesus
       b) Challenges to us from Christ's divinity

---

* The introduction has been omitted.

      3. True Human Being — for us today
        a) The image of true humanity
        b) Challenges to us from Christ's humanity

B. Jesus Christ — suffered and crucified for our sake

    I. The theme
   II. The Creed
  III. The biblical witness
  IV. Christ's suffering and death for us

C. Jesus Christ — his rule today and tomorrow

    I. The theme
   II. The Creed
      1. The Lord who is and who is to come
      2. The spring of joy and hope
  III. The biblical witness and later interpretations
      1. The relation between resurrection, ascension and Christ's rule
      2. The interpretation of the resurrection
  IV. The Risen Christ — today and tomorrow
      1. Christ's rule today
      2. Christ's rule tomorrow

A. JESUS CHRIST — TRUE GOD AND TRUE HUMAN BEING

I. The theme

1. The church is a community confessing, worshipping and serving Jesus Christ as Lord. This *confession* includes many dimensions of our belief and life: we proclaim that by the life, death and resurrection of Jesus, we are made citizens of a new world, God's kingdom; that we are set free from the tyranny of a past marked by guilt, violence and brought together by the victory of Jesus over all the powers enslaving the world; and that we are given the freedom and authority to call the God of Jesus our Father and to depend totally on his compassionate faithfulness. Thus the church confesses Jesus Christ as the image of the one true God, whom he called his Father. At the same time he is confessed as the image of true human being for whose salvation he became incarnate.

Since 1910, the ecumenical movement has rested on the basis of a confession of Jesus Christ as God and Saviour as it is explicitly expressed in the Basis of the World Council of Churches. But at a time when the nature both of God and of salvation is much in question inside and outside the churches, there is a pressing need to explore for our day that faith which found classical expression in the accounts of Jesus Christ as embodying a divine life "of one being with the Father" as well as a human individuality, "complete in all things belonging to us human beings" (Athanasius).

II. The Creed

> We believe in one Lord, Jesus Christ,
> the only Son of God,
> eternally begotten of the Father,
> Light from Light,
> true God from true God,
> begotten, not made,
> of one Being with the Father.
> Through Him all things were made.
> For us and for our salvation
> He came down from Heaven:
> by the power of the Holy Spirit
> He became incarnate from the Virgin Mary
> and was made man.

2. It is no accident that the second article forms the longest section of our Creed. In it is expressed the very heart of Christian belief and indeed of Christian identity. It elaborates what is involved in the simple act of Christian commitment to Jesus and to the Father of Jesus.

Its detailed formulations about Christ as incarnate Son of God have to be understood in the context of the fourth century's theological debates. The theological crisis of the fourth century was not strictly speaking about "the incarnation". All parties agreed that Jesus was not exhaustively to be described or understood as a human being; what was at issue was the nature of what became incarnate.

Arius had claimed that God's complete freedom and transcendence could only be asserted if it was stressed that God was the *only* eternal, self-sufficient being; he needs nothing other than himself, and has no natural relation to anything other than himself. Thus, although God may *choose* to become Father, and so choose to bring into being a Son, this relationship is not part of what it is to be God.

1. OF ONE BEING WITH THE FATHER

3. The second article of the Creed affirms the Lord Jesus Christ to be "the only Son of God". The phrases "Light from Light", "true God from true God" which follow this represent credal formulae, already in existence, clarifying this Sonship. All are of interest and significance, but the central — and originally most controversial — expression is the *homoousion* — "of one being with the Father".

This phrase was introduced by the first Ecumenical Council at Nicea in 325 as a safeguard against the view of Arius and his supporters. Against this, the Council affirmed that the relation of God as Father to the Son or word manifested in Jesus was a relation intrinsic and necessary to the divine being. God is not God in any other way but as Father and Son together in relationship, in a perfect mutual loving and giving and a perfect harmony of act and will.

Jesus Christ embodies for us the totality of a love responding to the gift of love, and so embodies the unique relationship between the eternal Son and the eternal Father. This free self-giving by which Jesus realizes in human history the life of God is the destiny to which we as human beings are called. And as Jesus in his self-giving receives full authority from the Father for the realization of his kingdom in healing, judgment and mercy, so we in him are enabled to realize this divine life and action in the world.

2. FOR OUR SALVATION HE BECAME INCARNATE

4. The second article of the Creed affirms also that the Only Son of God, who is of the same being with the Father, came down from heaven. He became incarnate for us and for our salvation from the Virgin Mary by the power of the Holy Spirit, and was made a human being. The Creed confesses that the Son who is eternally of the same being with the eternal Father became in time, by incarnation, of the same being with us mortals.

The fathers have explicated the mystery of the incarnation by the affirmation that it was realized in Jesus by the *hypostatic union* of God the Son with the humanity which He assumed. By this they meant that God the Son and the humanity were so united in Jesus that the union was perfect and real, neither the divine nor the human being confused with, or divided from, the other.

God the Son became really a *human being*. He shared fully all human conditions within the historical realm, never being led into sin that alienates us from God, though he was tempted as we human beings are. He underwent all human experiences of joy and sorrow, fellowship and privation, all the time being in himself fully composed and leading others to human fullness and divine glory. Through his humanity that is united with his divinity he elevates all those who believe in him to a divine life. By living in the world under its limitations, sufferings and conflicts, he showed us the way to a life of courage and strength, in the midst of the many vicissitudes that confront us every day.

The faith affirmed in the Creed shows us a soteriological perspective and the *goal* towards which we should move in our life on earth. Our life today is often unhealthy and unedifying as much to us as to others, so that we need to undergo a drastic change. In Jesus we have the *model* on which to pattern our lives and come to our real nature. Thus Jesus challenges all misguided life and aspirations of the world, demanding every human being to take up his way and move towards our final fulfilment and glory in him, through him and with him.

3. TOWARDS CHRISTOLOGICAL CONVERGENCE

5. As a sign of our growing convergence in understanding Jesus Christ as true God and true Human Being we refer finally to two agreed statements on Christology from earlier times. Already in 1967, representatives of the Oriental and the Eastern Orthodox Churches *agreed* in Bristol on the following statement:

> God's infinite love for mankind, by which He has both created and saved us, is our starting point for apprehending the mystery of the union of perfect Godhead and perfect manhood in our Lord Jesus Christ. It is for our salvation that God the word became one of us. Thus He who is consubstantial with the Father became by the incarnation consubstantial also with us. By his infinite grace God has called us to attain to his uncreated glory. God became by nature man that man may become by grace God. The manhood of Christ thus reveals and realizes the true vocation of man. God draws us into fullness of communion with himself in the body of Christ, that we may be transfigured from glory to glory. It is in this soteriological perspective that we have approached the Christological question.[1]

On 23 June 1984, Pope John Paul II and the Syrian Orthodox Patriarch of Antioch, His Holiness Moran Mar Ignatius Zakka I Iwas, signed in Rome a *Joint Declaration* which declares amongst other things:

> Hence we wish to reaffirm solemnly our profession of common faith in the incarnation of our Lord Jesus Christ . . . We confess that he became incarnate for us, taking to himself a real body with a rational soul. He shared our humanity in all

things except sin. We confess that our Lord and our God, our Saviour and the King of all, Jesus Christ, is perfect God as to his divinity and perfect man as to his humanity. In him his divinity is united to humanity. This union is real, perfect, without blending or mingling, without confusion, without alteration, without division, without the least separation. He who is God eternal and indivisible became visible in the flesh and took the form of servant. In him are united, in a real, perfect indivisible and inseparable way, divinity and humanity, and in him all their properties are present and active.[2]

III. The biblical witness

We are given a many-faceted and rich portrayal of Jesus Christ in the New Testament.

1. THE SON OF GOD

a) The unique relationship between Jesus and his heavenly Father (Synoptics)
6. What features of the gospel record point us towards the affirmation of a unique response by Jesus to God as Father? There are several points in the Synoptic Gospels at which we glimpse something of how the first Christians understood Jesus' prayer: he prays in the night and the early morning in solitude (Mark 1:35–36, 6:45–46); and he calls God by the intimate word "Abba" (Mark 14:36). It is probably this aramaic word that lies behind Jesus' persistent and distinctive reference to God as "my Father" in the gospel.

It is important to note that when we speak of "Father" and "Son" in their relationship to each other in the Trinity, we do not mean to imply that God is male. As a human being, Jesus Christ *is* male. But within the persons of the Trinity, there is no gender. The meaning of Jesus' relation to God as Father must also be understood as it appears and develops in the incident and narrative of the Gospels.

(1) Jesus' unique relationship to his Father is initiated by Mary's obedient reception of the angel Gabriel (Luke 1:38) and his *announcement* that she should bear a son who would be called "the son of the most High" (Luke 1:31), "son of God" (Luke 1:35). The Creed's phrase "born of the Virgin Mary" tells us both of his human *birth*, of a woman, and of the way in which God the Father is uniquely his father.

(2) Luke 2:49 takes us back to Jesus' *boyhood*: even here, the evangelist suggests, when there is a conflict between obedience to earthly and to divine authority, Jesus instinctively turns to "his Father's business" — a foreshadowing of the bitter conflicts ahead, when loyalty to the Father costs more and more, and yet is never set aside.

(3) And in the *baptism* stories (Mark 1:11; Matt. 3:17; Luke 3:22), the voice from heaven, "Thou art my Son, my Beloved" (or, as in Matthew, "This is my Son"), reminds us that the Sonship of Jesus is concrete vocation, an anointing and empowering in the circumstances of his human life as it unfolds — not merely a reality completed in his birth, a static "given".

(4) To this vocation, Jesus *responds* with joyful praise (Matt. 11:27): he experiences the Father's calling as a deep and ever-present intimacy of knowledge. And this knowledge, this complete confidence and familiarity with the hidden purpose of the Father, is dramatically expressed in terms of the judgment at the end of time (Matt. 10:32): in the presence of the Father, Jesus will determine the fate of human beings, according to their response to his call and proclamation. Response to Jesus will decide God's response to us.

(5) Jesus thus stands for the beginning and the climax of Israel's history — with Moses, who first interpreted the mind of God in the Torah, and with Elijah, whose coming heralds the last (Mal. 4:5). So Jesus is revealed in glory between Moses and Elijah, and yet he is revealed as more than Moses or Elijah: Peter identifies him as "the Christ, the Son of the Living God" (Matt. 16:16). At the *transfiguration* a voice from heaven again declares him "beloved" or "only" son (Mark 9:7; Matt. 17:5; Luke 9:35). But the climax in which the Son's authority and oneness with the Father are revealed is no simple apocalyptic victory: it is the exodus, "his departure, which he was to accomplish at Jerusalem" (Luke 9:31).

(6) The climax of the *last days* lies in the fact that when God has sent his Son, when he has fully expressed his fatherly love in Jesus, he has no more to give. "He had still one other, a beloved son" (Mark 12:6). When the rebellious tenants of God's vineyard reject the son, they reject their last hope, and bring the crisis of God's judgment upon themselves.

(7) The Son's task is to bear in anguish and solitude the ultimate rejection of those to whom he came: in a world refusing grace, he carries the weight and violence of that refusal, and cries, "Abba, Father" in the very moment when the meaning of his terrible destiny is clearest to him in *Gethsemane*.

(8) So, on the *cross*, he recognizes that he still has authority to intercede, even beyond human rejection, for the loveless and the violent. So rooted is he still in his Father's life that he can do no other than demand mercy for his torturers from the Father whose mind he so fully knows to be a purpose of grace and love (Luke 23:34). He dies trustfully commending himself to his Father (Luke 23:46) — an insight which is not cancelled but enhanced by the tradition of his cry of dereliction (Mark 15:34). It is appropriate that after this last manifestation of Jesus' Sonship, the Roman centurion should say, "Truly this man was a son of God!" (Mark 15:39; Matt. 27:54) — words with a stronger and deeper meaning than their speaker knew.

(9) As he dies in the name and for the sake of the Father's authority, the authority of the promise of mercy and life, so that same authority vindicates him. It is not extinguished by sin, rejection and death: the promise and the hope abide. And so Jesus is *raised* and given back to the world by the Father; and he is now authorized to send "the Father's promised gift" upon his followers, the fullness of life and the consequent power for preaching and witness that will come with the sending of the spirit (Luke 24:49).

The Synoptics thus fill out in narrative detail the great theme at the heart of the whole gospel: Jesus of Nazareth is the true son of God.

b) The divine authority in the public ministry of Jesus (Synoptics)

7. But how is it that Jesus' relationship to the Father becomes visible to others, an authoritative sign of hope to them? John the Baptist pleads for reassurance: "Are you the one who is to come?" And Jesus' answer (Matt. 11:4–6) gives the classical foundation for all Christology: "Go and tell John what you hear and see: the blind receive their sight and the lame walk, lepers are cleansed and the deaf hear, and the dead are raised up, and the poor have good news preached to them. And blessed is he who takes no offence at me."

Jesus answers John by pointing to the signs of the *kingdom's* presence, freedom, newness, fulfilment. His whole mission rests on the proclamation of the kingdom (Mark 1:15): God's moment is here, the kingdom is (if not wholly present) "among" the people (Luke 17:21), it has "come upon" them (Matt. 12:28; Luke

11:20). Jesus' presence effects, makes real, the triumph of God, his overcoming of all that resists him.

(1) It is a time of *fulfilment*. The Law is brought to completion, its demands are perfected and made intelligible by Jesus (Matt. 5:17–20). He is free to make radical qualifications and reinterpretations to bring out the full sense of the Law (Matt. 5:21–48; Mark 2:23–28, 3:4; Luke 13:10–17). He is not simply an exegete of the written word, but "speaks with authority" (Mark 1:27), unlike the qualified religious elite (Mark 1:22; Matt. 7:29; cf. Mark 7:1–13). He grasps decisively what it is to be doing God's will, and those who learn from him are his true kin (Mark 3:31–35).

(2) It is a time of *celebration*. The bridegroom is present: there can be no fasting or mourning (Mark 2:18–20; cf. Matt. 11:16–19). The feast which will celebrate the coming of God's rule (Luke 13:29, 14:7–24) begins now (cf. Luke. 15: 22–24). And it begins with the extending of God's welcome to the outcast and guilty as Jesus sits down to eat with them and be welcomed by them (Mark 2:15–17; Luke 19:9–10). It is effectively symbolized also in the feeding of the multitudes who turn to Jesus for material as well as spiritual nourishment. So more generally it is a time of welcome. Those whom Law of custom had kept on the edges of society or excluded from the chosen race are brought in along with the ancient people of God (Luke 13:29; Mark 7:24–30; Matt. 8:5–13). Women are treated as examples of faith (Matt. 15:28) and as potential disciples, with a right to meditative learning (Luke 10:38–42). Children are also held up as examples (Matt. 18:1–7, 10) and greeted with warmth (Mark 10:13–16).

(3) It is a time of *battle and victory*. Apart from the feeding of the hungry and the healing of the diseased, it is especially the casting out of demons that proclaims the kingdom's presence (Matt. 12:28; Luke 11:20). "The unclean spirits submit" to Jesus' authority (Mark 1:27). All that rebels against God in enslaving and crippling women and men is overcome (Luke 13:16), and Satan falls "like lightning from heaven" (Luke 10:18). The spirits recognize their master and yield (Mark 1:23–26, 5:6–13).

(4) It is a time of *forgiveness*. There is, as we have seen, a welcome for those despised and condemned, there is a recognition that thankful love for God can only spring from the experience of forgiveness (Luke 7:47). Above all, Jesus claims the *right* to forgive, to anticipate God's own judgment (Luke 7:48–50; Mark 2:1–12).

(5) And it is a time of *new life* — not only in the experience of healing, deliverance and reconciliation, but in the restoring of the dead to life, the swift and powerful response to the agony of loss (Mark 5:22–43; Luke 7:11–17). God is once again shown to be effective in the midst of his people, "visiting" them to manifest his re-creating power (Luke 7:16).

The time of Jesus is "the year of the Lord's favour": God's anointed, empowered in God's spirit, comes to effect pardon and release, *to make God present*, especially to those imprisoned or shut out by the sense of God's absence (Matt. 11:28). Jesus' union with the One he calls Father is shown in the fact that he has the authority to cause "God's moment" to happen. His time is God's time.

c) The eternal word of God (John)

8. St *John's Gospel* underlines as well the unique relationship between Father and Son and makes it even more exclusive: only the one who has come from God has seen the Father (6:46). There is also the other aspect of divine authority in the

life of Jesus emphasized in St John: in order to assure the sheep that nobody will snatch them from his care, the good shepherd declares: "I and the Father are one" (10:30). This claiming equality with God brings Jesus in strong conflict with some Jewish authorities (5:18). While they refuse to acknowledge his divine authority as God's only son (3:16f.), one of the twelve disciples, the doubting Thomas, confesses after the encounter with the risen Christ: "My Lord and my God!" (20:28). As a consequence of this, the famous prologue of St John's Gospel declares: "the only Son from the Father" (1:14) as the eternal word which "was with God at the beginning, and through him all things came to be" (1:2f, RSV).

d) The self-giving love unto death (Paul)

9. *Paul* quotes in his letter many sentences from the very early Christian tradition in order to demonstrate that his interpretation of the Gospel is in line with the very beginnings of Christianity. One early hymn about Christ speaks about his "divine nature" and his "equality with God" (Phil. 2:6). Another early formula declares Christ as Son of God "by his resurrection from the dead" (Rom. 1:4). Paul himself underlines especially the self-giving love of the Son of God unto death on the cross (Rom. 8:32; Gal. 2:20; Phil. 2:8). Based on the mighty act of resurrection from the dead Paul says that in Christ "the whole fullness of deity dwells bodily" (Col. 2:9). In this sense Christ is "the image of the invisible God" (Col. 1:15) and as a consequence of this he is understood as Lord over place and time: "for in him all things were created, in heaven and on earth, visible and invisible . . . he is before all things, and in him all things hold together" (Col. 1:16–17). It is rather unlikely that the Jew Paul of Tarsus should have given the full title "God" to Christ, as some exegetes interpret Romans 9:5, but certainly he ascribed to the one Lord Jesus Christ creative and saving power, "through whom are all things and through whom we exist" (1 Cor. 8:6).

e) The stamp of God's very being (Hebrews)

10. The solem introitus of the letter to the *Hebrews* which has so much to say about Christ's true humanity begins with a forceful praise· of the Son of God. Because he had brought about by his death the purification from our sins and is seated at the right hand of the heavenly majesty in the power of his resurrection, Jesus Christ is praised as "the glory of God and bears the very stamp of his nature" (Heb. 1:3). The Son has opened after many prophets the final age, he was made the heir to the whole universe and he sustains it by his word of power (1:1–4).

In conclusion one is allowed to say that the Nicene formula "of one being with the Father" has good grounds in the manifold New Testament witness.

2. THE HUMANITY OF JESUS OF NAZARETH

a) Sharing in the human condition (Synoptics)

11. (1) Jesus Christ was among us as one of us. He shared with us in *historical existence in time and place* (Luke 2:1–2). He was neither a myth nor a superhuman hero. He had a clear birthday, was born of a woman (Luke 2:7), and the time, place, and conditions of his death are known to us. Like all of us, he endured the limitations of physical life: he was born into a human family (Luke 8:19); he underwent an ordinary human development, growing from childhood into adulthood (Luke 2:40). He suffered the limitations of human ignorance. Jesus of Nazareth lived out his life in the circles of his family, his disciples, Jerusalem and

the Jewish people, and finally in conflict with the oppressive forces of the Roman Empire by which he came to his death.

(2) He was born and reared in a *Jewish culture and tradition* (Luke 2:21) which remained his the whole of his life (Luke 23:46). He was born of the line of David the king (Luke 1:27). As a Jewish male baby he was circumcized (Luke 2:21–24) and presented in the temple as the first born. He participated in the Jewish life of worship and celebrated its festivals (Luke 2:41–43; Mark 14:12). He loved the temple and was angry that it was defiled by money-changers and traders (Matt. 21:12–13). His religious convictions had their roots in the Jewish understanding of the Oneness of God and the radical claim God makes upon us (Mark 12:29–30) that we love God and live a life in accordance with God's grace to God's people. He fulfilled the obligations of a Jewish citizen under Roman rule, including the paying of taxes (Matt. 17:24–27).

(3) He shared with us an ordinary life of *human needs and emotions*. In the Gospel we see him thirsty and hungry (Matt. 4:2), tired (Matt. 8:4) and in pain. He felt compassion for the sick (Matt. 14:14), the suffering (Luke 7:21) and the grieving (Luke 19:41). He loved children (Matt. 19:13–14). He enjoyed eating and drinking (Luke 7:36) and visiting with friends like Mary and Martha. We see him feeling fear and mortal anguish at Gethsemane. He sometimes grew angry and he often needed solitude (Luke 6:12; Mark 1:35f.).

(4) He also knew *real temptation*, and the possibility of sin was not far from him (Matt. 4:1–2). In the desert he could have escaped from his true mission by succumbing to the temptations of money, power, and personal aggrandisement (Matt. 4:3–11). At Gethsemane, in his fear and mortal anguish, he was tempted to abandon his mission. He did not go like a hero to his death from the beginning, but had to learn obedience (Matt. 26:39–42). "If it be possible, let this cup pass from me, yet not my will but thine be done."

(5) It is significant that he was an *outcast* already at his birth, born in a stable among strangers (Luke 2:5–7). In his early childhood he was subjected to oppression as his family fled to exile in Egypt (Matt. 2:14–15). He grew up in the family of a carpenter, rather than as a member of an elite class (Luke 2:39–40, 57). He was not a scholar or a religious official of any kind. The ten commandments and the twofold commandment (Matt. 23:37–40) of love provided the basis of his work among the poor and outcast. He associated with tax collectors (Luke 2:15), "sinners", Samaritans, gentiles, women, children. He lived as a poor man without a home, dependent upon the charity of others. When he died, it was the shameful and physically excruciating death of a slave, upon a cross (Luke 18:32; Mark 15:25).

Jesus Christ experienced human life in all its aspects, physical and mental, personal, religious, cultural, sociological, and in his death the political.

b) The sending of the Son into the world (John)

12. *St John's Gospel* interprets in addition the human life of Jesus as God's sending of his only Son into the world (3:15f.; 17:3). His coming into the world does not primarily refer to his birth — John, like Mark, does not tell any birth story of Jesus — but rather to his mission on earth for the salvation of the world (3:17). John underlines especially that it is the Son of God who came down from heaven, thus pointing to the love of his heavenly father (3:16). The earthly origin of the "son of Joseph" creates problems only for those who do not trust him as "bread from heaven" (6:41f.). The prologue goes in the same direction and follows

an antidocetic intention when it speaks about the word which became flesh, dwelling amongst human beings in glory, full of grace and truth (1:14).

c) The other Adam (Paul)

13. The pre-Pauline hymn for Christ mentions not only the "human likeness" of Jesus Christ; it emphasizes rather more the paradox that the one equal with God "emptied himself, taking the form of a servant, being born in the likeness of men" (Phil. 2:7f.). Paul himself follows the same line of real humanity underlining that God's own son was "born of woman, born under the law" (Gal. 4:4) and died "on a cross" (Phil. 2:8). Paul's interpretation of Christ's true humanity reaches its deepest and at the same time its most universal level when he speaks about its relevance for the whole humankind: Christ is the other Adam, who overcomes the disobedience, unrighteousness and sin of the first. His true humanity represents the new humankind. "Then as one man's trespass led to condemnation for all men, so one man's act of righteousness leads to acquittal and life for all men" (Rom. 5:18). The old and the new Adam contradict each other like death and life: "For as in Adam all die, so also in Christ shall all be made alive" (1 Cor. 15:22).

d) The learning of obedience through suffering (Hebrews)

14. We find in the letter to the *Hebrews* the same pointing to Christ's likeness with all human beings "in every respect" (2:17; 4:15) as in the very early Christian tradition. That means for this letter especially his being tempted (4:15) and the test of suffering (2:18). In very realistic terms the letter speaks about "loud cries and tears" during the days of his earthly life (5:7). His being the son of God does not contradict his learning of obedience "through what he suffered" because suffering belongs to his true humanity.

For the New Testament both aspects, Christ's sonship and his true humanity, do not compete with each other; rather, they complement and interpret each other. Divine authority and human suffering belong inseparately together in the life of the one person Jesus Christ.

IV. Jesus Christ: true God and true human being for us today

1. CONTEMPORARY EXPERIENCES

a) Concerning Jesus of Nazareth

15. It is amazing enough that Jesus of Nazareth who lived and died almost 2000 years ago belongs today to the best-known persons in the world. There are not very many people who have not heard at all about a person named Jesus. Instead there are very many people who appreciate him as teacher like Mahatma Gandhi, as prophet like Mohammed, as revolutionary like the Marxists, as reformer of our life-style like the youth movements, as peace-maker like the peace movements etc. It is a very positive aspect that the person Jesus of Nazareth attracts so many people in such different perspectives.

More problematic is the fact that Christians who claim Jesus Christ for themselves understand him often in a contradictory sense which contributes to separations among Christ's disciples. Others regard him often just as one model of life amongst others like Karl Marx, Che Guevara, Mahatma Gandhi. It is without any doubt a big challenge to the Christian faith to identify the true human being Jesus of Nazareth in such a way that he unifies his disciples and helps to answer the burning questions of our time.

b) Concerning God

16. It is much more difficult for millions of people today to understand Jesus as the only Son of God and to relate him to his Father, in other words to find through him the true God as the New Testament witnesses do. Today the contrary is in manifold ways the case: the human being Jesus of Nazareth comes close whereas God whom he claimed as his father becomes more and more distant. More than ever is the very existence of God for many people an open, unsolved question. There are broad branches of atheistic theories like most of the existentialist thinking, there are atheistic ideologies which call the attention of millions of people as in Eastern Europe, there exists first of all an atheistic practice in many parts of the modern world. The great challenge to the Christian faith in this regard is to witness through Christ to God's present reality in such a way that people begin again to believe in his merciful reality.

c) Concerning our human being

17. As a consequence of two world wars, of high living standards, of growing secularism and pluralism a tremendous crisis of meaning of life has taken place in the second half of our century. Sometimes developments end up with a paradox. It seems to be true for many people: the more economic welfare they win, the more meaning of life they lose. The growing number of persons committing suicide, especially in Western countries, is an alarm clock which can no longer be ignored. Here the Christian faith is challenged to confess the person Jesus Christ in such a way that people can regain meaning for their personal and public life through the experience of the God whom Jesus confessed as his father in whose name he brought salvation to our threatened world.

2. True God — for us today

a) The God of Jesus

18. (1) Jesus Christ appears to us a historical human individual who nonetheless acts out of a unique sense of relationship to *God as Father*, a relationship that gives him authority to make real in history the victorious compassion of God. His "place" in our world is God's; he is the image in history of a decisive power resourceful enough to make and remake the world.

So we can say that in Jesus God is shown in a *definite* way. And if this is true, the God of Jesus is, quite simply, *God*. We can have no language for him that is not the language of Jesus — the language of Father and Son acting in harmony and love. The creed is right to insist that God is not God independently of his being Father. His being is in relation: Jesus comes to be seen as a "translation" into human history of an eternal response of perfect love and praise to an eternal initiative of overflowing life and reality.

(2) God, then, is a *unity-in-diversity*. He is neither an eternal individual, *nor* a "group" of eternal individuals; both models are impossibly static, artificial and anthropomorphic. He is living act, diffusing itself, reflecting and answering itself, sharing itself. To enter the life of God is to enter through Jesus, at the point where God's love responds to its own fullness, and to be enabled, in the Spirit, to communicate it as we grow in it.

(3) To say anything short of this would be for us, as Christians, to jeopardize our belief in *one* God. If we believe that the time of Jesus is a time of fulfilment, not total discontinuity, we must believe that the God of the Old Covenant at last fully reveals in Jesus what is foreshadowed and hinted at in the history of Israel.

(4) The power of God, as we meet it in Jesus, is defined as essentially a power-making for our *salvation*. God does not need to "decide" (let alone be persuaded) to be *our* God. The life that flows from him is a life destined to be shared by his creatures. The divine authority given to Jesus is the authority to spend himself to the utmost, to die and to rise, *for us*. God has indeed no more to give (Mark 12:6). "As the Father has life-giving power in himself, so has the Son, by the Father's gift."

If God is by nature not only Father but liberator and redeemer, it is possible to see that the affirmation of Jesus as "true God" expresses the foundational Christian belief that God's saving act is prior to all our decisions and all our deserving. The meaning of Trinity is interwoven with our commitment to "justification by faith" rather than by our own works apart from the Christ.

(5) All our reflection on God as Trinity rests on the experience of the kingdom, the experience of renewed humanity. The theologians of the early church were right to appeal to the baptismal formula in their defence of the Creed, because it is in *baptism* that we make our own the kingdom, the new creation. In the name of Father, Son and Holy Spirit, we claim "the promised gift", our inheritance as God's children. By sharing the cross and resurrection of Jesus, the image of God's life in our world, we find in him the image of our humanity restored. In Christ, "of one being with the Father" and "complete in all that belongs to us as human beings", we are once again reconciled to the source and end of all that is.

b) Challenges to us from Christ's divinity

19. (1) To confess Jesus Christ as son of God challenges an attitude which regards him as only one important person amongst others. It rather implies to affirm him as "the way, and the truth, and the life" (John 14:6). Thus he challenges *our full trust* in him.

(2) Since Jesus makes God present in the world *our approach to God* is challenged. God is not to be found far away beyond or behind our reality, rather in time and place, in our world and history. "The word is near you, on your lips and in your heart . . . " (Rom. 10:8).

(3) There is no theoretical way to prove without any doubt the *existence of God*. Jesus calls instead for obedience and discipleship: "If any man's will is to do his will, he shall know whether the teaching is from God or whether I am speaking on my own authority" (John 7:17).

(4) Jesus' reinforcement of the first commandment challenges the *false gods* of our daily life: trust in self-reliance, money, economic welfare, arms race etc. Martin Luther explains the first commandment: "Where your heart is, there is your God."

(5) Christians share the confession to the one, undivided God with Jews and Muslims. They challenge *other religions* like Hinduism in India which adore many gods and incarnations.

3. TRUE HUMAN BEING — FOR US TODAY

a) The image of true humanity

20. (1) Confessing Jesus Christ as the truly human means first of all to affirm his sharing in the *conditions of normal human life*, its gifts as well as its limitations, its

chances as well as its temptations. As a human being Jesus of Nazareth was able to undergo all basic human experiences: from his birth in a stable in the village of Bethlehem until his death on a cross outside the gates of the holy city of Jerusalem; from celebrating feasts with great joy to suffering under the torture of Roman soldiers.

It is of great help for us today that Jesus shared our human conditions. As the Epistle to the Hebrews (2:17) puts it: "Therefore he had to be made like his brethren (and sisters) in every respect, so that he might become merciful." The likeness of Jesus Christ "in every respect" means that he is with us in every human situation as a merciful Lord, be it in the joy of a wedding feast or in the pain of a prison.

(2) Sharing in the general human conditions does not mean that Jesus lived out his life like everybody else. On the contrary: the difference between his life and ours is that he learned to be obedient to his Father in every respect (cf. Heb. 5:8). "For we have not a high priest who is unable to sympathize with our weaknesses, but one who in every respect has been tempted as we are, yet without sin" (Heb. 4:15). Being tempted belongs to our general human condition, but to overcome temptations *"without sin"* is unique in the earthly life of the Son of God. To live without sin "in every respect" means for Jesus basically not to focus on his own life rather than on the will of his Father and on the salvation of God's creation. In other words, the negative term "sinlessness" points to the positive fulfilment of God's first command: You shall love the Lord your God and your neighbour as yourself (cf. Mark 12:30f.).

(3) Thus his life lived under normal human conditions is the image of our truly human being; he is the *second Adam*. By his being and becoming, his words and deeds, his anger and his love he shows us for our salvation what our true human image looks like, what we should be and what we could become in the power of God's presence in our midst. Since he is able to convey his love "in every respect" and to keep doing so under the hardest pressure of human sin at the cross, he shows us the way to the overcoming of sin and death, how to correct self-centredness through love.

(4) The true human life of Jesus of Nazareth is not only a general and unattainable ideal for human beings but a concrete model for the realization of Christian *discipleship* in the power of the Holy Spirit. After having washed the feet of his disciples Jesus says to them: "I have given you an example, that you also should do as I have done to you . . . A servant is not greater than his master" (John 13:15f.). In general, his life points to the golden rule of love for our daily life. What this means under concrete circumstances of poverty, hatred, oppression etc., he shows us by his attitude towards the poor, the oppressing and oppressed people, thus giving us as his disciples a very concrete example for the direction and the way of life, in which we shall go in order to receive true life abundantly.

(5) Thus we understand the incarnate life of the one person Jesus Christ as the image of the one true God as well as the *image of our truly human being*. Being the only Son of God he brings into our midst the real presence of his Father, in order that we may become his children. Being the only image of true human being he grafts us into the tree of "Israel", he calls us as beloved children of his Father into his discipleship, he points forward to the renewed people of God in the church and he promises a new creation in which one humankind lives in one spirit as manifold children of his Father, the one true God. Therefore, the church adores and praises Jesus Christ as *vere Deus — vere homo*: true God and true Human Being.

b) Challenges to us from Christ's humanity

21. While self-centredness and lovelessness may be characteristic of human life as we know it, the humanity displayed to us in Jesus Christ challenges us to grow into a new and real humanity in the following ways:

(1) We must define the truly human by our *positive capabilities* that are meant to be ours as part of the image of God, not by our destructive capacities (cf. John 9:1–3).

(2) The historical rootedness of Jesus Christ asks that we take seriously our own *historical existence* within the whole people of God through the centuries and throughout the world as well as with humanity at large (Eph. 4:4–6; 1 Cor. 12:12–26; Matt. 1:1–17; Luke 1:26–27; Luke 3:32–38 etc.).

(3) Jesus' dependence upon his friends and his own care of others challenge us to understand that *dependence* upon and *responsibility* for others are part of our necessary humanness (Luke 10:38–42; 8:2; Rom. 15:1; Gal. 6:2; 1 John 4:7).

(4) Jesus' own *life-style* as well as his care for the poor and the social outcasts challenge us to disassociate productivity and the signs of wealth and worldly success from the definition of what it means to be fully human (cf. Matt. 19:16–26).

(5) Jesus' *celibate life* challenges us to see both marriage and celibacy as Christian options, and to understand sexuality not as an end in itself but rather belonging within the context of a shared life of love (cf. Matt. 19:1–12).

(6) Jesus' willingness to share in our *helplessness* and his ministry to the helpless challenge us to take our own *mortality* seriously and to acknowledge the full humanity of those who are not considered valuable by a society because of youth, age, illness or physical limitations (Luke 23:11; Mark 15:34–37; Luke 2:7).

(7) Jesus' humanity challenges us to fulfill human needs on the basis of the *value* of all human beings to God rather than in terms of rights (Matt. 25:31–46; cf. Matt. 9:35–36, 16:32).

(8) Jesus' own valuing of women as well as of men challenges us to recognize that in Christ there is *neither male nor female* and to live this Christian reality out in our churches, our homes, and our wider culture (Gal. 3:28; Matt. 15:22–28; Luke 9:36ff., 10:38ff.).

B. JESUS CHRIST—SUFFERED AND CRUCIFIED FOR OUR SAKE

I. The theme

1. Beginning with the early New Testament witness and throughout the centuries the church *confesses* that Jesus Christ suffered and was crucified for us. The theological significance and focus of this confession is indicated by *"for our sake"*. These words point to the decisive saving event for all human beings. Such confession is, of course, made on the basis and in the perspective of the full Christological confession of Jesus Christ being true God and true human being and of Jesus Christ being raised from the dead by God.

2. How can that apparently incredible, impossible confession that one person suffered and died for the whole of humanity of all ages be substantiated? How can the "for us" be interpreted and proclaimed in relation to the human condition of our time? Is it possible for churches of different traditions and living in diverse cultural, historical and socio-political contexts to be joined together in a common response to the above-mentioned and other *questions*?

II. The Creed

> For our sake he was crucified under Pontius Pilate;
> he suffered death and was buried.

3. In the Nicene-Constantinopolitan Creed the *crucifixion, suffering and burial* of Jesus Christ are the only data concerning his human history besides the fact of his birth. They sum up and denote the mission of his life which was aimed at our salvation. The reference to "suffering", following after the reference to "crucifixion", is related to Christ's death. This can be concluded not only when all the historical circumstances of this credal articulation are taken into account, but also when the various aspects of Christ's dying are considered.

4. The *death* of Christ in the Creed is given a comparatively brief reference when compared with the preceding section which deals with the Divine Person and the incarnation of Christ. This imbalance is readily understood when the context of the Arian controversy is taken into account; but it has a positive import, inasmuch as it makes it absolutely clear that he who was crucified and suffered and was buried was the eternal Son of God who became a human being. In this light the death of Christ reveals that God does not stand apart from the human predicament, nor does He meet it from a transcendent standpoint, but participates in it and thus provides the solution for it.

5. Particularly significant in this credal formulation is the phrase *"under Pontius Pilate"* which not only indicates that the death and suffering of the incarnate Son of God is a specific historical event but puts it in the wider context of world history and human political power.

6. The most significant phrase in the credal formulation of Christ's death is *"for our sake"* which also appears in the preceding formulation concerning the incarnation and indicates not just the significant link between the incarnation and the death of God's Son, but especially their saving character for all humanity.

7. Finally in the Creed Christ's death is fundamentally linked with Christ's resurrection, ascension and second coming and thereby opens up the dimension of Christ's saving victory over death on behalf of all humankind.

III. The biblical witness

8. Both the event and the meaning of the suffering and death of Christ are proclaimed in a variety of ways in all the writings which constitute the New Testament. The *Synoptic Gospels* see the suffering and death of Jesus as the inevitable and final consequence of his life and ministry. They indicate that Jesus' manner of life and his teaching brought him into conflict with the religious authorities and had political implications. The condemnation of Jesus by the Jewish religious authorities led to his execution by the Roman state. The Gospels also present Jesus' teaching his disciples about the necessity of his suffering and death in Jerusalem as presenting the will of God (Mark 8:31, 9:31, 10:32ff.). They show Jesus in seeking to do this will experiencing inner agony and struggle (Mark 14:39) and even a sense of utter abandonment (Mark 15:34). Ultimately Jesus' obedience in suffering and death results in the fulfilment of his Father's will, which finds expression in the gift of God's love to the world.

9. In the *Gospel of St John* Christ's suffering and death are given a wider meaning in the sense that they expose a deeper struggle between the God of love, light and life, and the world of evil, darkness and death, between belief and

unbelief (12:31, 14:30, 16:11,33). But all this is obviously related to the very person and the whole life of Jesus and to his victorious cross.

10. In the early preaching of the apostles as seen in the Book of the Acts, the suffering and death of Christ are interpreted with reference to the Old Testament prophetic imagery of the righteous servant (Acts 3:14), on the one hand, and on the other hand to the resurrection as the vindication of God's servant. The crucifixion is the prelude to the fulfilment of God's purposes in the resurrection. Here too, as in the Gospels, Christ's suffering and death have saving significance inasmuch as they imply that Christ suffered and died "for us".

11. The meaning of the suffering and death of Christ "for us" acquires further interpretation in the *Epistles*. In saying that "God gave his Son for us all" (Rom. 8:32) and in quoting an old credal confession, "Christ dies for our sins" (1 Cor. 15:3), St Paul interprets Christ's suffering and death in the light of Isaiah 53 which states: "He was wounded for our transgressions, he was bruised for our iniquities . . ." (53:5). The death of Jesus is of paradoxical nature: the one who was without sin was to carry our sins so that the sinful ones may receive forgiveness; the curse and death of the one in whom God came into our midst becomes a blessing for all (cf. Rom. 8:3; 2 Cor. 5:21; Gal. 3:13). The meaning of this "for us" or "for our sins" is presumably threefold: (1) our sins are the root cause of Jesus' suffering and dying; (2) Jesus Christ accepted representatively and vicariously for us the death which we ourselves really deserve on account of our sins; (3) Jesus Christ died for our liberation from death and sin and our justification by and before God. These are three aspects of one and the same event, of course, and are indissolubly bound up with one another. They interpret the death of Jesus in terms of the notion of expiation and representation. Because it is God who gives his Son, this expiatory event is God's action for our sake, an event in which God reconciles us to himself (2 Cor. 5:18).

It is a dying "*for us*", in the sense that Jesus, despite all the hostility and all the pain inflicted upon him by people and authorities, did not abandon his mission of love but persisted in it — the very same love in whose strength he displayed to his fellow human beings the unconditional love of the Father. Jesus' death is not a "condition" in the sense that the Father's love requires such an expiatory offering; rather Jesus' life was lived under such human "conditions" which made his death on the cross inescapable: it was inevitable that in bringing the Father's boundless love into this world Jesus had to suffer such demonstrations of hostility which led to his death. In this sense, then, Jesus' sacrifice in suffering and death is the means for bringing God's love to humanity. The notion of Christ's death as sacrifice which appears in Pauline teaching (Rom. 3:25) and in 1 Peter (1:18f.) is particularly developed in the Epistle to the Hebrews where Christ stands for us in obedience to God as our great high-priest.

12. The suffering and death of Christ as a saving event for us is *appropriated* by us in two ways which are closely inter-related. On the one hand through believing in the proclamation of the word, through receiving baptism as taking part in Christ's death and through partaking of the eucharist Christians are forgiven their sins and participate in the saving grace issuing out of Christ's vicarious suffering and death (1 Cor. 1:18; Rom. 6:3–5; 1 Cor. 11:23–25; Mark 14:22ff. and parallels). On the other hand, Christians participate in the suffering of Christ in following him in their life and bearing their cross (Mark 8:34; Heb. 12:2ff.). In Colossians 1:24 St Paul's sufferings are related in a mysterious way to Christ's suffering, as a "filling up of what is lacking in the sufferings of Christ for the church which is his

body". The New Testament teaching as a whole, however, underlines the uniqueness and sufficiency of Christ's suffering and death for the salvation of humanity. It is the continuing task of the church to confess, proclaim, celebrate and live this reality in obedient discipleship to its suffering, crucified — and risen and living — Lord, the head of his body.

IV. Christ's suffering and death for us

13. In continuity with the apostolic faith as witnessed by the holy scripture and summarized in the Nicene Creed, we *confess* today that Jesus Christ suffered and was crucified for us. This confession is made in a world which is marked as never before by the struggle between the forces of life and the forces of sin, suffering and death.

14. As at all times human beings are in bondage to sin. They are *estranged* from God and seek to justify themselves by their own efforts and achievements. This self-centredness, egoism and striving for power over others also manifest themselves in the attitudes of whole groups of people and in many contemporary social, political and economic structures.

15. Such human sinfulness is one of the root causes of *suffering and death* through lack of love, hatred, negligence, selfishness, domination and unjust or oppressive forms and conditions of life. Hunger, imposed poverty, exploitation, discrimination because of race, class, sex or political conviction, oppression by means of totalitarian and unjust systems and anxiety in the midst of an unprecedented arms race, ruthless exploitation of natural resources and an ever-widening gap between rich and poor nations are some of the consequences.

16. Individuals and groups of people *suffer* under alienation, hopelessness, despair, loneliness, illness and pain, corporal and mental handicaps or natural calamities. Such suffering may be self-inflicted or a reaction to the kind of societies and world we live in, or it may be experienced as an innocent or meaningless suffering. But there is also a freely accepted suffering because people continue today also to risk their lives in order to help and save others and to alleviate human suffering through their commitment to social change.

17. The lives of all human beings come to an end. All face *death*, unexpected and premature, caused by others, by suffering, illness, accidents or disasters, or they approach their own death and the death of loved ones as the conclusion of a long life. Death is the sign of our sinful, finite and passing world.

18. Yet despite all identifiable causes and rational explanations of suffering and death a deeper question remains: *Why is there suffering and death at all?* Why does this kind of suffering happen to me and not to others? Why are my people at the abyss of starvation while others are enjoying their affluence and apparent security? There seems to be no convincing answer in all attempts of human minds to wrestle with the mystery of suffering and death.

19. Behind these questions lies a hidden or open *protest* against suffering and death. This protest finds explicit expression in the struggle of the forces of life against the forces of sin, suffering and death. There is compassion with and sensitiveness for the suffering ones. Many efforts are undertaken in order to improve the conditions of human life through medical care, social services and through changing structures which inflict massive suffering and death. Religions, philosophies and ideologies seek in their way to sustain the struggle against suffering and death. We believe, however, that the forces of life find their most firm

roots and overcoming strength in the suffering, death and resurrection of Jesus Christ.

20. The *gospel* of the suffering and death of Christ is good news for all people, not only those who actually suffer but those who seem to be free from it, for the sick as well as the healthy. All human beings live in a situation of sin and death and are in need of Christ's redeeming grace. Indeed, the entire creation groans and travails awaiting the salvation of humankind (Rom. 8:19). The salvation offered through the suffering and death of Christ does not explain the why of human sin, suffering and death, but shows how it is overcome.

21. The death of Christ has been understood in three ways which have come to be regarded as "classical":

a) The *first* type of interpretation is found in the theology of the ancient church and is continued in the tradition of the *Eastern* church in particular. Here, the death of Jesus Christ — God and human being — is seen as destroying death's power and influence by which human beings are burdened and oppressed. The death and resurrection of Jesus is a victory by which human beings are liberated from death and all the powers of darkness.

b) A *second* type of interpretation is found in the Latin *West*. Here the death of Jesus is understood as an atoning event whereby the guilt incurred by human beings in God's sight because of their sin is expunged.

c) There is a *third* type of interpretation which is found especially in *modern* theology. Here the dying of Jesus is seen in the perspective of his total obedience. He remained faithful to his mission right to the very end. Thereby he became for us the example and even prototype of a life which refuses to be diverted from its devotion to God and other human beings and which claims God as the loving and merciful one.

On the basis of the biblical witness as outlined above we believe that these interpretations are not alternatives. They emphasize particular aspects of that witness and should be held together as complementary.

22. Christ suffered and died for the liberation of humanity from the grip of sin and the judgment of God upon it. *Sin* opposes and alienates human beings from God and also from one another. It causes hatred and suffering among human beings, gives rise to unjust and oppressive institutions and structures in human society and leads the human being to disturb the natural world order. This situation created by sin is also to be seen as a manifestation of God's judgment, in that, as the apostle says, "he gives humanity up to uncleanness through the lusts of their own hearts" (Rom. 1:24, cf. 26 and 28).

Christ came into this situation of sin and of God's judgment. In his suffering and death he experienced the consequences of human sin. He was sent by God "in the likeness of sinful flesh and for sin" (Rom. 8:3) as one who was himself without sin, as lamb of God (John 1:29) and he carried away the sins of the world like a scapegoat (Lev. 16:22).

This was the way in which God was reconciling the world with himself and saved it from sin and judgment. The message of the *reconciliation* accomplished in the death of Jesus is for all people the offer of liberation: through justification and forgiveness of sins received in faith as well as in the gift of new life from the Holy Spirit. God is comforting consciences burdened by sin and guilt. He liberates people from the devilish circle of self-justification and egoism, hatred and injury to the neighbour, lack of gratitude towards God and disregard of God.

God calls and empowers human beings to effect reconciliation with each other both as individuals and as communities. Reconciliation is possible in that people have been liberated from themselves and learn to respect the right of others, also of those of different convictions, and see in them people who are also loved by God.

23. Christ suffered and died on the cross as the incarnate Son of God. In the suffering and cross of Jesus, God has taken upon himself human pain and death. God demonstrated his solidarity with and his compassion for human suffering. This was not done in order to justify suffering and death or even make them into something divine, rather to declare war on them and to *overcome* them by the way to the victory of the resurrection. God is on the side of human beings in the struggle with the powers of sin and death.

This has a twofold meaning for people who are under sin, suffering and death. God is demonstrating to them that he is with them in these situations, that he is suffering where people are suffering and is thereby giving them consolation and strength. God is also providing them with a hope for a life which is no longer marked by death. On the other hand God's solidarity empowers human beings to struggle against sin, suffering and death, against all forms of injustice, exploitation, oppression, war, racism, etc.

24. Because Christians are incorporated into Christ, they are led in many ways to suffer with him in participating in his obedience. The call to *discipleship* implies the readiness to carry his cross, because the "yes" to God today runs the risk of entering into the destiny of Jesus Christ, of his "yes" to God for which he was crucified.

And in our *suffering for others*, Christ uses this suffering to do his work of love and salvation through us. Such suffering with Christ for others has marked the life of many Christians, beginning with the followers of Jesus in the first Christian communities through the centuries till today. This company of suffering witnesses includes the many well-known martyrs as well as millions of unknown Christians. Through their participation in Christ's suffering they received the gift of new life which overcomes all suffering, and they witnessed to this gift to their fellow human beings.

25. The suffering and the apparent scandal of the crucifixion of Jesus exposes and *unmasks* the unjust powers of this world. The one who was innocent and just was crucified as a criminal, and this scandalon continues in history to unmask injustice that tries to appear as justice. The crucifixion of Jesus also exposes the cruelty of human beings and of dominant religions and political powers. They seemed to triumph over the only righteous and loving one. Yet their victory was revealed as defeat by God's victory in the resurrection. What appeared to be strong, legal and established was exposed as weak and penultimate. The apparent weakness of God proved to be stronger than the mighty ones.

All Christians and churches are, therefore, called to continue in the power of Christ's suffering, crucifixion and resurrection to unmask the inhuman and oppressive powers in this world. Looking back at those who pretended to serve God's will by crucifying his Son, Christians are enabled to identify the *idols of today* which try to take the place of the true and only God. This critical attitude includes an awareness over against the danger of a false triumphalism in the church and among Christians which overshadows God's victory in the cross and resurrection of his Son. Rather, Christians are called and empowered by their obedient suffering with Christ as well as in explicitly denouncing all powers that seek to take the place of God to be effective witnesses to Jesus Christ, the life of the world.

C. JESUS CHRIST—HIS RULE TODAY AND TOMORROW

I. The theme

1. The believers experience the presence of the living Christ in their worship services, in celebrating the eucharist, in accepting and in offering forgiveness, in loving and in blessing one another. They would not be able to pray, were it not in the name of Christ. They would have no hope in this world of death and hatred, were it not for their belief that the suffering Christ is *the Risen One*. By this they mean that Jesus Christ has been vindicated by God and that their own future, their freedom before God and the world, depends on this vindication and victory. They can do this because they know that the Servant–Lord is present in their sufferings and difficulties, indeed that he participates in the struggles of the people towards a God-willed and truly human future. As adopted children of God, they can freely review and discuss their own past—history with all its failures and sins—because they know of forgiveness. They can also openly and fearlessly face the future because they rely on the promise of God that his shalom and righteousness will indeed be the final word on human history and on the universe.

II. The Creed

> On the third day he rose again
> in accordance with the scriptures;
> he ascended into heaven
> and is seated at the right hand of the Father.
> He will come again in glory to judge the living and the dead,
> and his kingdom will have no end.

2. These affirmations are the *sources for* the believers' *joy and hope*. The Creed's statements in this part consist almost entirely of direct and indirect quotations from New Testament texts. The purpose of this selection of central biblical affirmations must be seen in the original use of Creeds in baptism. In later centuries as well as today, these summarizing statements express in doxological language, i.e. in language primarily addressed to God in worship, the heart of the Christians' joy and hope for themselves and for all creatures in the ongoing high-priestly work of Jesus Christ.

1. THE LORD WHO IS AND WHO IS TO COME

3. The affirmations of the Nicene-Constantinopolitan Creed of 381 which refer to the resurrection, ascension and to the present as well as eternal rule of Christ follow a *chronological* order. In this they continue with the pattern found in the first half of the Christological article of the Creed. Thus the Creed reflects a vision of the "history of salvation", similar to earlier and shorter creeds in the Eastern and the Western church, e.g. the Apostles' Creed. This is of particular importance with regard to the statements concerning the second advent of Christ and the final consummation. History will reach its end, his rule will not. It is noteworthy that the concept of a millenium, a reign of 1000 years following the second advent, is absent. (It had already been discarded by Hippolytus in the early third century.)

4. This section of the Nicene-Constantinopolitan Creed reflects the fact that the church had settled the question as to whether God the Father or God the Son was to be seen as final judge. There is biblical evidence for either of these views. The risen Jesus Christ is the judge.

Of special interest is also the explanatory addition to the affirmation of the resurrection: "according to the scriptures" (1 Cor. 15:3). Whilst the Creed affirms Christ's crucifixion as an event "for us", a corresponding phrase with regard to the resurrection is not expressed. Rather our justification is connected with the final judgment.

2. THE SPRING OF JOY AND HOPE

5. The resurrection of Jesus Christ is a present reality, and not a mere past event. It makes its presence felt in various ways and manners, though in a veiled form in this present age. In fact, it is the ground of Christian joy as well as hope.

The resurrection of Jesus Christ gives rise to *joy* which expresses itself in the joyful singing of hymns and lyrics, in liturgical and extempore prayers — collective as well as individual — in the celebration of the eucharist, in Christian fellowship, in search for a wider and deeper Christian unity, in sharing the good news of Jesus Christ even in adverse circumstances, in service to the poor, the needy and the sick, and in Christian giving. For the resurrection of Jesus Christ liberates us from the forces of death, makes our justification possible as well as meaningful, and assures us of the continued presence of Christ in all situations and in every circumstance. It is the joyous message of the resurrection that enables Christians to cross all human frontiers and break all human-made barriers: caste, class, race and sex.

6. The resurrection of Jesus Christ also evokes *hope* in us — hope for the life on earth as well as life beyond death. For it points to a wider horizon and to God's offer of a new future, both for the individual and the whole humanity. In the light of the resurrection, therefore, there are no ultimate dead-ends or hopeless situations, because the God of the resurrection is present in Christ to offer a new possibility, calling forth life out of death. This hope drives away the fear of death and all evil powers. It refuses to be satisfied with maintaining the status quo of the old creation and challenges all oppressive powers that thwart new life. The life that is based on the resurrection concerns itself with the wholeness of human personality, knowing full well that it is not only the spiritual but also the physical that matters. At the same time it seeks the wellbeing of the neighbour and the renewal of humanity since it knows that Jesus rose again to be the new head of humanity.

7. This hope enables us to work for *changes* — both in the church and in society at large — in so far as these changes are positive and liberating. It also gives us strength to accept suffering in the name of Christ, whether it is imposed upon us against our will or whether it is voluntarily chosen for the sake of others. In all these situations it is the Risen Lord who brings peace that surpasses all understanding and cannot be taken away. As Jesus' resurrection was God's act of vindication of what Jesus said, did and stood for, the belief and hope that are based on the resurrection challenges the church to stand by the side of the oppressed, the marginalized and the deprived, and to work for justice concerns. The church needs to take this challenge seriously, so that it may not fall into the danger of a false triumphalism.

The resurrection of Jesus Christ is, thus, the spring of Christian joy as well as hope.

III. The biblical witness and later interpretations

1. THE RELATION BETWEEN RESURRECTION, ASCENSION AND CHRIST'S RULE

8. The Creed fully represents the intimate connection between the resurrection, the ascension and the present and future rule of Jesus Christ as it is expressed in

theological passages, in admonitions as well as in the doxological parts of the New Testament. The biblical witness is undoubtedly unanimous in stressing the unity of these realities, although *differences* are found among the individual books in the New Testament in the emphasis on the distinction between them. Whilst, for instance, the distinction between the resurrection and the ascension is not mentioned in the writings of the apostle Paul, and not stressed particularly in the Gospel of St John, Luke/Acts emphasize a chronological sequence in which the ascension followed Easter after forty days. This latter chronology has become the dominant view in the early church and is expressed in the Nicene-Constantinopolitan Creed.

9. The *presence* of the risen Jesus Christ among the worshipping community (Matt. 28:17), even outside the church in complex human situations, and indeed in the individual lives of the believers (Gal. 2:20), is central to the explications and exhortations of the New Testament. This presence is at times expressed in terms of the earlier Jewish understanding of the *shekinah* of God, at times in sacrificial language but also in terms not used before the coming of Jesus Christ. The epistle to the Hebrews speaks of the ongoing intercession of Christ the High Priest.

10. The New Testament passages concerning the *Last Judgment* follow Old Testament or apocalyptic writings. They all presuppose the identity of the Crucified Christ with the Risen One and never suggest that the judge is an unknown God who treats the believers as strangers.

11. All of these observations call for an examination of the meaning of *"the presence of Christ"*. We cannot explain the way in which Jesus of Nazareth absented himself from his disciples, nor can we compare the mode of his presence today with seemingly similar forms of spiritual presence, e.g. with the feeling which may emerge among the friends of a dead leader. The Risen Lord has his own mode of making himself present in the Holy Spirit. However, the inability to explain the mode of Jesus Christ's presence does not mean that the believers are incapable of pointing to signs of his presence in their congregations, their individual lives, and indeed in society and history in general. They search with the eyes of faith for such signs and rejoice in them. They also see the challenge to put up those signs themselves in spearheading a new humanity in justice and peace. Thus the resurrection and the ascension are fundamental for the Christian's social responsibility, not merely for their own piety or their hopes for life after death.

2. THE INTERPRETATION OF THE RESURRECTION

12. After the death of Jesus the disciples encountered the Risen Lord in a number of appearances. Those among the very early believers who were familiar with the *Old Testament* and especially with apocalypticism were prepared to grasp the proclamation that Jesus had been raised from the dead "according to the scriptures" (1 Cor. 15:3). Jesus as the first-born of the dead (15:20) was in an exemplary and unique way the recipient of the creative power of the God who calls light from darkness and life from death. Thus the New Testament passages which by direct or indirect reference to Old Testament or to apocalyptic writings refer to the resurrection, all reflect this particular event: Jesus is raised from the dead. This, however, is not to say that they all portray an identical understanding of this event. The differences range from the direct assertion that Jesus' dead body became alive in a form similar to his body before death (Luke 24) to the conception of a resurrection to a spiritual body (1 Cor. 15).

13. There was, however, another way of referring to the resurrection which seemed to have been geared to those *unfamiliar* with Jewish scriptures. Passages of this kind are found in the Gospel of St John (John 11:25) and especially in the brief, ancient hymn in 1 Timothy 3:16:

> He was manifested in the flesh
> vindicated in the Spirit,
> seen by angels,
> preached among the nations,
> believed on in the world,
> taken up in glory.

14. In addition to these varying articulations of the resurrection in the New Testament, *later theology* has provided a series of interpretations which deserve to be mentioned. They are not all mutually exclusive. Some of them, however, are wanting in the richness and fullness of the biblical Easter message. All of them intend to take seriously the ongoing work of God in Jesus Christ and the identity of the Crucified with the Christ who is present:

— The early church (in combatting Gnosticism) stressed the physical understanding of the resurrection, an understanding close to that of most of the biblical witnesses. Affirming the resurrection — this must be admitted — at times came close to affirming Easter as a verifying miracle.

— Gnostic as well as later philosophical interpretations often affirmed the entirely spiritual nature of the resurrection (the appearances of the risen Lord as visions).

— The concept that Jesus Christ was, so to speak, raised into the church and its authority structures, was not alien to certain tendencies in Western piety and theology.

— Related to this is a recent explication of the resurrection as the occurrence of "Jesus having been raised into the apostolic message of the church" (the kerygma).

— There is also an eschatological interpretation which refers to our inability to demonstrate the historicity of the resurrection of Jesus. This interpretation stresses the fact that we "will know" how Jesus was raised and that such foreknowledge renders it probable that the Easter of the past was indeed a historical fact.

Whilst the believers today cannot fully agree on the mode of the resurrection, there is no disagreement among us on the confession that the resurrection of Jesus is the foundation of our lives — and that of the whole world — and the promise of our own resurrection.

IV. The Risen Christ — today and tomorrow

1. CHRIST'S RULE TODAY

15. In affirming Christ as Lord, "seated at the right hand of the Father", we affirm our faith that, in spite of human sin and all its painful consequences, God is and will be *victorious* over all the forces of evil and over death itself. This is the basis of the "good news", and of the ministry and mission of the church. We proclaim the gospel in order that Christ's reign may be extended in the world.

16. The Lordship of Christ is not merely an objective or impersonal fact; it is an event which demands our *response*. In the Risen Lord we recognize the Servant

Lord, the Crucified One. He calls us to be faithful disciples, to continue his ministry of loving service, to take up our cross and to suffer for his sake. It is in so doing that we participate in the new creation which began at the first Easter. Mere intellectual or ritualistic affirmation of Christ's Lordship belittles this high calling.

17. In the Nicene Creed, Christians proclaim that the forces of death and evil have been defeated, that Christ now reigns with the Father, and that God's kingdom of peace, justice and love is already a reality. This affirmation seems to be in strong contrast to human *experience* in a world in which we know evil and suffering in many forms, and in which all life ends in death. In the light of such experience Christians may repeat Job's questioning of God. They may feel powerless and hopeless when confronted with the many problems of our world and the enormity of suffering. But we see in the resurrection ground for our faith that God is the one who calls life from death. Faith in the resurrection and in the power of the Resurrected One gives us a new perspective from which to view our experience in this world. It is *in spite of* evil, suffering and death, that we proclaim Christ as Lord.

18. In the present age we still await the fulfilment of Christ's victory and reign, but with the eyes of faith we see signs of the resurrection present in our midst, wherever new life breaks into the old. We see *resurrection signs* in the lives of men and women who fearlessly commit themselves to follow the Crucified One, and in the witness of the many martyrs of our time. We see many signs wherever there is new self-understanding and new sense of community, wherever healing, reconciliation and liberation take place, wherever there is openness to change and growth. We experience foretastes of resurrection whenever faith in Christ, hope in Christ, and love in Christ lead us to such openness.

19. This faith helps us to overcome our human fear of death and suffering. As the risen Christ gave peace to his fearful disciples and enabled them to move out from behind closed doors into a hostile world, so he gives us peace, and with it the *courage* to be and to move out joyfully from behind our closed doors into the many possibilities of new life.

2. CHRIST'S RULE TOMORROW

20. As Christians we are united in our conviction that we all have to appear before the *judgment of Christ*. There are however differing beliefs about the time and manner of Christ's return and of the judgment. There are some who affirm a realized eschatology, to whom judgment is a present experience, while others have a more apocalyptic understanding, believing that the end-time and the judgment are yet to come. Some believe in individual resurrection of the dead; others believe that judgment will occur only at this universal resurrection. For many of us, this diversity of Christian understanding reflects a diversity within the New Testament writings, in which we distinguish both the Johannine perspective and that of the author of Luke/Acts, as well as the shifting Pauline interpretation.

21. The formulation in the Nicene Creed that Christ "will come again in glory to judge the living and the dead" does not take into account all the traditions which are contained in the New Testament. In particular, in its proclamation of Christ as the judge, it ignores the traditions in which Christ is the *advocate* who pleads on our behalf as we stand before the judgment of the Father, and in which Christ is himself the sacrifice for our sins. We believe that the manifold images used by the biblical writers are indeed *images* and that we should not imprison them within juridical language and conceptuality.

22. The temptation of Christians is often to set ourselves up in judgment of others, or to desire a *divine Judge* who will judge according to *our* will. However we believe that the "good news" is that we are not called upon to judge. This does not mean that we are to refrain from creative social criticism and political action. But judgment is God's prerogative and will take place according to God's will as revealed in Christ. As such, it may well have outcomes different from what we expect and desire.

23. As far as God's judgment on *us* is concerned, we agree in our belief that, however much *righteousness and love* may be in tension in human life, the full witness of the Bible is that in God they cannot be separated. We are not righteous, but our judge is the righteous one. We cannot abdicate our human responsibility for our sin, but we face our judgment trusting in God's merciful and forgiving love, revealed to us in the Christ who himself has gone through suffering and vindication, and teaches us to love our enemies.

24. In proclaiming that "Christ will *come again*" we affirm our faith that history will not end in chaos, but that it will end in the One in whom it had its beginning, the One who is the Alpha and the Omega. We recognize that there is a tension between realized and apocalyptic eschatology, but we all believe that the new creation began in Christ will also be fulfilled in Christ. We understand this as an all-inclusive fulfilment, for our individual justification and salvation is only part of the longed-for redemption of the whole creation. So we join ourselves to the intercessory ministry of Christ, praying for the unity of the church and the renewal of human community.

25. Thus we *wait* in eager hope for the final fulfilment and consummation of God's offer of new life, which is given to our world and history in the resurrection of Christ, the Crucified, the Lord. "Beloved, we are God's children now; it does not yet appear what we shall be, but we know that when he appears we shall be like him; for we shall see him as he is" (1 John 3:2).

NOTES

1. In "Apostolic Faith Today: a Handbook for Study", H.-G. Link ed., *Faith and Order Paper No. 124*, Geneva, WCC, 1985, p.166.
2. In *L'Osservatore Romano*, English edition, 2 July 1984, p.7.

We Believe in One Lord Jesus Christ

Interpretation of the Second Article of the Creed:
the Way from Kottayam to Potsdam

DIETRICH RITSCHL

Introduction

The task the Faith and Order Commission has set itself in the programme "Towards the Common Expression of the Apostolic Faith Today" is not, strictly speaking, the interpretation of the Nicene-Constantinopolitan Creed (which we shall call, for simplicity's sake, the Nicene Creed). The Nicene Creed is to serve as basis and signpost to simplify the task of the representatives of the various member churches of the WCC as they seek to articulate the contents and structure of their common faith. The Creed is to act as a guidebook, mapping out the contents to be discussed together, indicating the sequence of the main doctrinal themes to be dealt with and—though this goes beyond the function of a guidebook—to be read and treated with the seriousness it deserves as the only ecumenical Creed of Christendom. For undoubtedly, among all the creeds adopted by an ecumenical or other important synod, the Nicene Creed is the only one which has been accepted as fundamental by all the main churches which have subsequently emerged.

That is not to say that there are not other churches, denominations and church fellowships which since their inception have deliberately dispensed with the reception of fixed doctrinal formulations and therefore assign to them no special place or no place at all, even to the Nicene Creed. When the decision was taken in the Faith and Order Commission to undertake a study of the Nicene Creed, the representatives of these denominations were confronted with considerable problems. This is not the place to discuss these difficulties, but it should not be forgotten that the representatives of the mainline churches and smaller denominations who are now involved in the programme do not all attach the same importance to the task of interpretation they have set themselves. For the Orthodox family of Eastern churches it is axiomatic that any legitimate interpretation of the faith of Christians must be based on the Nicene Creed and on the other ecumenical councils, whereas the churches of the West are not as strict in their view of the binding authority of the Nicene Creed. The way the work has gone so far, however, shows that fruitful and solid cooperation is still possible even where there is no fundamental accord on the authority of the Nicene Creed.

Actual work on the programme began with the three consultations, including the one held at Kottayam, Kerala, on the second article of the Nicene Creed. But useful work had already been done even before the three consultations set to work, each concentrating on one of the three articles of the Creed. This preliminary work was familiar to the members of the three consultations and influenced at least the defining of the task. In some respects it also affected the formation of the contents. Thus the members of the small consultation in Kottayam were furnished with a carefully assembled body of material beginning with texts from the Lausanne conference of 1927, through Edinburgh 1937, Lund 1952, down to the latest consultations in Klingenthal 1979, Princeton and Odessa 1981 as well as Rome 1983. These texts were meant to orient the work of the consultation. At the same time, the Geneva staff of Faith and Order had produced a proposal for the structuring of the discussion and the texts to be drafted. Once again the importance of this kind of preparation was demonstrated, since every theological consultation runs a risk of being vexed by the wealth of themes relevant to its work and interconnected in such a complex way.

The Kottayam consultation took place from 14 to 22 November 1984. The score or so of participants were guests of the Malankara Syrian Orthodox Church and worked in the Sophia Centre in an excellent atmosphere strongly influenced by the liturgical life of the seminarists as well as the consultation's own worship, by the generous hospitality also of other churches in the city and by the ambiance in India shortly after the assassination of Indira Gandhi.

In what follows I shall describe the course taken by the interpretation of the second article of the Nicene Creed from Kottayam down to its most recent revision in West Berlin and in Potsdam. We shall need to keep in mind the following stages in the drafting of the text:

A) consultation in Kottayam (14 to 22 November 1984);

B) revision of the A text in Geneva by a small group assisted by the Geneva staff of Faith and Order (9 to 11 April 1985);

C) the draft for Stavanger, produced in Crêt-Bérard, June 1985 (this can be labelled the *Crêt-Bérard I* text);

D) the adoption of criticisms and suggestions from the study groups in Stavanger (August 1985) and individual contributions again in Crêt-Bérard and Geneva in March/April 1986 (this can be labelled the *Crêt-Bérard II* text);

E) the most recent text (provisional), based on Crêt-Bérard II, and produced at the meeting of the Standing Commission in West Berlin (9 to 12 July 1986) and Potsdam (13 to 19 July 1986).

In the Ecumenical Institute of the University of Heidelberg we have undertaken a complete comparison of the various texts. The findings of this research cannot be presented in their entirety here, of course. I shall have to confine myself in this report to the main themes and the alterations in their presentation. The tripartite division which was already a feature of the Kottayam text and which has been adhered to since was helpful here. In each of the three sections of the report, I shall describe the development from Kottayam to Potsdam in essence, i.e. pointing out important alterations and additions. The bare two years of the history and development of the text reflect the movements from the spontaneous and the unguarded to the doctrinally cautious and systematic style of discourse, in many respects characteristic of church history and the history of doctrine generally. The incisive changes and expansions appear in the C and D texts, whereas the E text (Berlin/Potsdam) seems at first to register few changes or none from the D text, but then radically alters the D text (37–51 and 68–76). Text E seems on the whole to have been drafted so unevenly and hastily that the following report can concentrate in the main, without much loss, on the changes between A and C and between A and D.

I. The incarnation — interpreted in terms of the salvation of the world

1. General aspects of the evolution of the text

Structurally, the text produced in Kottayam (A) adopted the proposals made in Geneva for an arrangement and definition of themes. In A the *vere deus—vere homo*, the whole idea of incarnation, was regarded as a fundamental theological problem and as an essential confession of faith, discussed more or less carefully in the light of biblical texts and examined in the context of the cultural and religious situation in India. There was a rich input from the history of doctrine. Already in B, however, and then still more clearly in C, the doctrinal note begins to predominate. Various additions are then found in D and the emphasis begins to shift to the *vere deus*. In this first section, E is identical to D. The procedure originally planned, i.e. from the situation to the text of the Creed and from that to the biblical basis, could not be adhered to completely in the later development. It was also called in question in Stavanger. This raises an important problem, of course. In the confession of the common faith, should we proceed from the Bible, via the Creed of the ancient church, to the contemporary situation? Or should we proceed the other way round? Since text B, "Creed and Biblical Basis" has been consistently summarized in a first section followed by a second section on "Explication for Today". Similarly, since B, in each of these sections there is often a small-print section headed "Commentary". This pattern has been adhered to down to the E text of Berlin/Potsdam. The dominant impression that it gives is that in these texts it is a question of interpreting the Nicene Creed in form of an exegesis of the content followed by an "application" for today. It may be questioned whether this is faithful to the original intention.

2. Input from lectures

Individual lectures given at the Kottayam consultation had been prepared in advance and designed to serve as a stimulus. The lecture given by *Prof. Roberta C. Bondi*, an American Methodist, deserves to be singled out for special mention. Her topic was the *vere deus—vere homo* in the religious and cultural context of America. She dealt interestingly with the problems of asserting the "true humanity" of Jesus. Being more at home with "non-literal" uses of language in the field of "religion", Americans had difficulties in taking the "full humanity" of Jesus literally. Language in the church is dominated by a docetic trait. The question of the male identity of Jesus was also discussed. Prof. Bondi, being a patristic scholar, spoke in a way our hosts found easy to comprehend even if they also had difficulties in understanding the references to the specifically American situation.

B. H. Jackayya, an Indian Lutheran, dealt with the Asian context of the Christian life and Christian creed. He adopted an authentically biblical approach and showed no eagerness to accommodate it syncretistically to Indian notions of incarnation.

Dr R. Perera, an Anglican from Sri Lanka, raised questions of a deeply political kind throughout the consultation, specifically in respect of the proclamation of the gospel and its efficacy. He called for ways of coming to terms with Buddhism which is the dominant religion in Sri Lanka, though without indicating what these might be.

Dr V. O. Jathanna of the Church of South India seemed to find it easier to develop clarifying concepts for distinguishing between Christian views of incarnation and corresponding Hindu concepts. The papers read by *Prof. Ulrich Kühn* (Leipzig/Vienna) and *Dr M. J. Joseph*, Mar Thoma Syrian Church, Kottayam, related to the subjects discussed in this report under sections II (the passion) and III (the victory over all powers).

Also important were the comments contributed by *Ms Vimla Subaiya* of Calcutta, though these were available in written form to the members of the consultation only some weeks later. Ms Subaiya is the head of a large boarding school in Calcutta which has educated influential Indian personalities. She deplored the connection of Western influences and colonialism with the gospel and sought to show the difficulties of proclaiming the gospel in a way which goes to the very heart of the Hindu tradition. In an impressive way, she combined thoughts about Jesus, his humanity and his mission, with insights into the need in India to present the presence and life of the God of the Bible through Christian communities. Her paper also discussed ways in which the life of the Hindu has been changed by the influence of Christians. Ms Subaiya also sees the incarnation of God in Jesus Christ as a challenge to Indian Christians to enter into serious dialogue and exchange with Hindus and people of other religions. The work of the consultation was greatly enriched by the spiritual authority and commanding wisdom of Prof. V.C. Samuel, of the Orthodox Syrian Church of the East (Kottayam and Bangalore).

3. The Kottayam text

As we have said, the Kottayam text adopted the tripartite division already proposed by Geneva and, in the section covered here, deals with the clauses of the Creed from "We believe in one Lord Jesus Christ . . . ." to ". . . of the Virgin Mary, and was made man". Attention focuses, therefore, on the questions of the *homoousia*, the becoming human "for our salvation", and the motherhood of Mary. At first there seemed to be few differences over the ancient church formulas and their interpretation. It was only later that differences arose over the understanding of these texts between the Greek theologian George Dragas (who teaches in Durham, England) and myself (despite our long-standing acquaintance). The main point was the appraisal of the truth content of dogmas: are they receptacles or containers of truth, or do they regulate the discourse of believers concerning the truth? The discussion led to a very happy understanding. Not surprisingly, it was in respect of the *homoousios* and the *theotokos*, in particular, that the difficulties were recognized. Although exegetical observations played a considerable part in the discussions in Kottayam, there were only sporadic references to biblical texts. The evaluation of biblical and ancient church statements about salvation remained unequal: are they to be taken to refer to forgiveness, to deliverance from death, or as having a political reference in the sense of liberation and wholeness of life? In almost all the discussions, the true humanity of Jesus was viewed in the light of human suffering on the Indian sub-continent and in other countries where hunger is predominant. The discussions and also the Kottayam text itself thus acquired a pastoral dimension which receives less prominence in the later texts, especially C and D. Feminist concerns as well as questions of marriage and celibacy came under consideration. The responses of other religions to challenges in the field of social ethics were also kept in view in the discussions.

4. Additions and deletions (Crêt-Bérard I)

Text C expands the preamble (in 2) by adding a long list of questions intended for clarification. The biblical and historical material (4–12) is tightened up and systematized. At the same time, the explanatory sections on the Creed (13–16) assume a more apodictic and academic style. They then came under criticism also in Stavanger, though without being improved in D and E. Some parts from text A have dropped out, especially the passages which speak graphically of the true humanity/humanness of Jesus and refer to his life and ministry.

5. Development in the direction of a doctrinal text (Crêt-Bérard II and Potsdam)

The list we have made of omissions and additions in D as compared with A and B is in many respects alarming. That is not to say, of course, that text A was richer than the later texts but it is clear that the additions in text D (identical in the later text E) are almost exclusively concerned with scholastic distinctions and add nothing new in substance. This applies especially to the systematization in 1, the addition in 2 (already found in C), the explanation of the *homoousios* in 5, the abridgment and addition in 7, the substitution of the new paragraphs 8 and 9 for earlier sections, as well as to additions in 10–15. These sections are clearly concerned to explain synoptic passages (8–11) in respect of the *vere deus—vere homo*, as well as Johannine (12) and Pauline passages from the epistles. It can safely be said, on the whole, that the method of starting in the first place from the text of the Nicene Creed and then putting questions to the biblical texts has been maintained. The only question is whether the evident increase of detailed arguments and specific biblical references in texts D and E does not make it necessary to undertake a far more extensive and comprehensive exegetical, historical and systematic presentation. In other words, it could well be that a shorter and more spontaneous text would fulfill the purpose of the Faith and Order project better than a relatively fuller and more methodical text which falls between two stools, being beyond the comprehension of those untrained in theology but on the other hand appearing too meagre for the trained theologian. When we read the D and E texts, we feel the need to read not ten pages but a substantially longer text on the relationship of the incarnation to the salvation of the world, one which really discusses in detail the questions raised. But that would certainly not be what the Faith and Order project intends.

II. The passion — the suffering of God and humanity

1. General aspects of the evolution of the text

The themes of the texts in this second section of the second article of the Nicene Creed are: the crucifixion under Pontius Pilate, the death and burial of Jesus. The language of the Creed here follows the chronology of historical events. The interpretation of these credal clauses raises all the themes of the doctrine of reconciliation of classic theology. Whereas in the discussion at Kottayam, a contribution made by the English theologian *Rowan Williams* on the question of the *vere deus — vere homo*, in which he strongly emphasized the findings of synoptic and Johannine scholarship, enabled his working group to make a very detailed report on the first theme, the text on the second theme of the Christological article is rather shorter and less oriented on biblical exegesis. This need not necessarily have been so, but resulted from the nature of the discussion, and also and especially from the relative absence of theological differences at this point. *Prof. Ulrich Kühn* tried to explain the vicarious sufferings and death of Jesus Christ in a paper but his argument presupposed the situation of German-speaking theology rather than the ancient church background which was more familiar to our Orthodox hosts and the Roman Catholic members of the consultation.

The later texts faithfully reflect the A text, though with a number of additions, which were certainly necessary to make good obvious gaps in the argument of the A text. On the other hand, the political dimensions still noticeable in Kottayam take a back seat in the later texts. Even in texts D and E there is no real "theology of God's solidarity with human suffering". In all the texts from A to E we likewise miss a clear answer to the delicate question of whether, and if so in what sense, it is possible to speak of the "sacrificial death" of Jesus without subscribing to the notion of a "payment" to God through the death of Jesus, a concept which finds hardly any support today. This is a "delicate" question because conservative evangelicals make it the decisive issue between "orthodox" believers and the rest, but also because theologians of the Eastern Orthodox Church, as well as those of the Roman Catholic Church, employ the terminology of sacrifice without acknowledging that they are speaking metaphorically.

2. Sensitivity to the cultural dimension

One impressive feature in Kottayam was the constant awareness of and reference to the cultural and social problems of the Indian sub-continent and questions arising therefrom. It is impossible to divorce the theme of the sufferings of Jesus, God's solidarity with humanity's sufferings in the sufferings of Jesus Christ, the abandonment by God which Jesus experienced, and the gospel of his death, from the despair and sufferings of human beings on this continent and in many other parts of the world. Theological statements about the passion of Christ remain abstract, hackneyed and insipid unless they bring out clearly the profound inner connections that exist here. Whereas until quite recently European churches and European theology were represented by people who had first-hand experience of human suffering in the Second World War, in the last ten to twenty years or so the voice of those who represent the suffering and impotence of people in the countries of the third and fourth worlds has been increasingly in evidence in official ecumenical circles. In the discussions in Kottayam, therefore, the different approaches to and methods of dealing with all this suffering were also considered explicitly: the victory over suffering by way of negation and the striving for extinction, as in the ancient Asian traditions, and, in contrast to that, the Old and New Testament message of God's participation in suffering with a view to victory over it and newness of life. Here there are real differences between the biblically based faith and some important Eastern religions which are otherwise in many respects similar to the biblical tradition. Recognition of this fact strongly influenced the discussions in Kottayam even if it did not find its way clearly enough into the Kottayam text.

3. Difficulties over method in Kottayam

Brief reference must once again be made to the substantial differences between the representatives of Eastern Orthodoxy and those of Western theology. In respect of method, it is not at all clear in our ecumenical work in general whether we should start from established dogmas (e.g. the dogmatic formulas of the ecumenical councils) or whether we should retrace and re-examine the doctrinal development in the light of the biblical evidence. It is really not a question of the *sola scriptura* principle (so often made central) in opposition to the strategy of beginning with the Tradition or placing it on an equal footing with the Bible. In contemporary systematic theology this is no longer the real or the realistic alternative. The question is rather whether we decide to approach the great questions of the faith by arguing on the basis of the ancient texts (i.e. the Bible *and* the ancient church Creeds) or, on the contrary, on the basis of our contemporary questionings. As theologians, are we to "make the Bible relevant for today" or should we not rather make present events, developments and questions "relevant" for the rudiments and bases of our faith and our history, which leads from Abraham through Jesus' sufferings, death and resurrection down to ourselves? These difficulties about method were discussed in Kottayam without any firm agreement being reached.

4. Additions and alterations before Stavanger

Whereas text A begins with theological questions arising from the Nicene Creed and only afterwards turns to the biblical witness, the C text begins with biblical and historical references. The specification of biblical passages must necessarily be very selective. The *pro nobis* is strongly underlined. In none of the texts from A to E do we find any explanation of what it really means to assert that a man who died two thousand years ago really died "for us". This shows once more the degree to which these ecumenical texts are already operating within a Christian system of thought and how frequently they retreat from basic and quite essential questions, regarding them as already solved.

Nor is it clear how far Christians can believe and confess that "the death of Jesus" was "willed by God" even though it is clearly stated that Christians have always opposed the interpretation of the death of Jesus as a tragedy. The text does not bring out clearly enough that the death of Jesus was not a private death but that his burial was a "private" burial, and that therefore his burial was meant to confirm the reality of his death and was not as such vicarious in character. These facts, though clear to biblical scholars and even to systematic theologians today, have not found any reflection in the texts. Towards the conclusion of their remarks, all the texts — including the E text (55 and 56) — show a tendency to celebrate Jesus' death as a victory over evil forces. In other words, the death of Jesus is quite clearly interpreted in the light of Easter; as a result of this, it seems almost to acquire a docetic character in the C, D and E texts. The statements about this victory achieved through the crucifixion of Jesus are disappointingly stereotyped in all the texts and almost nowhere explanatory.

5. Unanswered exegetical questions

Most of the difficulties have already been mentioned implicitly. Did the death of Jesus involve a sacrifice? How are we to explain the ambivalent position of Judas as, on the one hand, a traitor and, on the other hand, a "go-between" or deliverer? To what extent is it certain that the death of Jesus was not a "tragedy"? Was his death, namely, his readiness to accept it, a prayer, a "self-sacrifice" or an offering in the sense of a gift which human beings are to bring to God? What have we to say about the exegetically demonstrable differences between the Pauline letters and, for example, the First Epistle of John? In respect of the death of Jesus, how is the implicit Christology of Hebrews related to the Pauline letters and the Synoptic Gospels? And lastly: to what extent are we to interpret the death of Jesus as qualitatively different from the death of Mahatma Gandhi or Martin Luther King? Does the difference lie exclusively in the resurrection or is it also — as British theology and certainly large sections of the American church tradition, too, would want to maintain — in the life of Jesus that the difference lies? These questions have only been touched on in passing in the texts.

6. The influence of the work in Stavanger

As a result mainly of the criticisms contributed by *Prof. Raymond Brown*, the American Roman Catholic New Testament scholar, a whole series of exegetical statements in texts B and C were called in question. His exegetical comments referred in particular to the true humanity of Jesus, to the recognition of his unique authority by those who heard him, and, generally, to an anti-docetic interpretation of the relevant biblical passages. From a theological standpoint, Brown emphasized the connection between the raising of Jesus and justification and offered a summary of the findings of scholarship, already familiar to European and especially to German-speaking scholars, on "becoming new" and "new life" through the resurrection of Jesus. The critical report of the working group which criticized the C text (Crêt-Bérard I) adopted Brown's exegetical desiderata as well as the theological criticisms made by George Dragas and myself. The working group called for a complete revision of this C text in respect of the original purpose and outlined a fresh draft. As sequence for the revision, it also proposed the following steps: firstly, explanatory comments on the text of the Creed; then reference to biblical passages; and finally, an examination of the application for today. These proposals have now been adopted in texts D and E, although the disadvantages of text C complained of in Stavanger have only partly been remedied. Texts D and E are terribly doctrinal, include very little discussion of practical questions and problems and on the whole strive for an internal theological coherence which may be praiseworthy but is in certain ways inherently tedious in its effect.

7. *Additions in Crêt-Bérard II*

While, therefore, texts D and E do contain some clarifications and improvements in comparison with the earlier texts, they have on the whole a colourless effect and the truth is replaced by a whole set of platitudes. That may seem a harsh verdict but one has only to read §§37 to 56 of the D text (the draft for Potsdam) to wonder whether this is really the way we Christians want to speak of this central doctrine, i.e. that Jesus suffered and died for us. We are not blaming anyone for this; but it is nonetheless lamentable that nuanced figures of speech arrived at in joint ecumenical efforts should seem to move in the direction of a common denominator which simply consists of a stringing together of conventional traditional Christian phrases. Nothing is "untrue" in these phrases, but little is true in them and little is clear. What is meant, for example, when it is stated in E.55 that: "The suffering and the apparent scandal of the crucifixion of Jesus exposes the unjust powers of this world"? Or again, that "the crucifixion of Jesus exposes the cruelty of human beings and of the dominant religious and political powers"? Or that "the justice of God condemns the injustice of all power that excludes and murders"?

III. The victory over all powers

1. *General aspects of the evolution of the text*

This third part of the section of the text of the second article deals with the clauses on the resurrection, the ascension into heaven and the sitting at the Father's right hand, the return to judge the living and the dead, and the doxological clause about the kingdom that has no end. It is little wonder that, already in Kottayam, these clauses of the Creed strongly encouraged the use of doxological language. The Orthodox hosts and the mere fact that they were more or less in a majority in Kottayam made it natural for particular attention to be paid to the importance of this doxological style. This note is still recognizable in the later texts even if it seems somewhat diminished in the D and E texts. The Kottayam text had been drafted by Janet Crawford, the Anglican theologian from New Zealand, and myself, and accepted at a pinch by the Orthodox and Roman Catholic members of the consultation. The difficulty lay in the fact that in our text we referred to the double language of Paul: in 1 Timothy 3:16, Paul is clearly addressing himself to Hellenistic readers, whereas in 1 Corinthians 15 he clearly has his eyes on readers familiar with the "scriptures" to which he can appeal. The result is that the resurrection is spoken of in different terms in each case. This double language was important to us in Kottayam but is only indirectly reflected in the later texts. In the later versions, there are numerous biblical references — indeed, by far the richest citation of the biblical evidence — so that what is said loses in clarity. This can easily be seen by reading §§62–65 of the E text where the reader is confronted with a whole set of biblical references but not with a statement or a confession of faith.

2. Regional and confessional conditions

What the Indian Christians were able to tell us in Kottayam about Hindu conceptions of resurrection and eternal life was of some importance. As was made very clear by Dr Jathanna in particular, these indigenous Christians clearly have to contend with a widespread tolerance in the religious context of Hinduism, a willingness to accept watered-down statements on resurrection and awakening. But what does it really mean to affirm that "Jesus was raised, awakened, from death"? In addition to these culturally caused difficulties of articulating the Christian faith, there are also confessional differences among Christians themselves. Whereas it is well known that the Eastern Orthodox Church traditions are accustomed to celebrating the resurrection in their doxology as a signal and evident "victory", in Western theology our discourse about the resurrection is defined more in terms of mystery or the veiling of a real act which it is impossible to present in human terms. On the other hand, those theologians who argue solely from the standpoint of political or liberation theology (Dr Perera of Sri Lanka represented this standpoint) tend to see the account of Jesus' resurrection more as a symbol of the liberation of the oppressed. An ecumenically responsible Christian theology really must insist on clarity here!

3. The Kottayam text

The Kottayam text can admittedly be regarded as a legitimate interpretation of the third part of the second article of the Nicene Creed only in a rudimentary sense. The doxological language, i.e. that mode of speaking which remembers that in all our speaking God is present and addressed, is to the forefront here. Assertory or apodictic statements have been avoided. Even the question of "Christ's lordship", therefore, is on the one hand a theme of doxological and expectant utterance but also, on the other hand, touches in a very direct way on the question of good or bad "rulers" in the contemporary world. In any case, the pronouncedly eschatological change in the language about lordship in the Nicene Creed demanded consideration. Is the "rule" of Christ to take place only after his "return in glory", i.e. after the "judgment", and are we, therefore, to think in terms of and to accept a chronological process? Or in what sense can we already speak today of God's rule over the world in Christ? These very important questions were certainly touched on but in no way answered. Yet they are of quite central importance for our search for a common confession of the apostolic faith today. It seems to me that we are not entitled in our project to avoid commenting on this central issue. It is also quite essential that we should tackle, and provide a responsible answer to, the specific concrete questions concerning the "judgment" which are repeatedly posed in the various churches. Only in a very incomplete way did that happen in Kottayam.

4. Later changes

The effort to come to grips with these questions is already recognizable in the B and C texts but what is said on them still remains extremely vague. A typological listing of the possible variations within the Christian tradition is the most that is attempted in many cases. The device of inserting brief commentaries, a method introduced from the B text onwards, is generally retained and should also continue to be useful in the further revision of the texts. The detailed commentaries so far formulated deal with some aspects of the difficulties of the themes in question here, but are still not by a long chalk a "common expression" of the apostolic faith. It may also be that a consensus in these questions is not possible; in that case, this must be frankly stated.

It seems to me that a whole set of individual, social-ethical and political questions are simultaneously involved in Christian discourse about the resurrection. There is firstly the question of individual life "after death" which is such a problem for us in our pastoral work, and then, of course, secondly, the question of how far "new life" is an indicator or a reflection of resurrection, in the medical field, for example, where cures, in a certain sense, are equivalent to something "new" emerging from the "old". What is a cure if not a sign of revival? And in the field of social ethics and politics: when love replaces hate, reconciliation conflict, what is that if not a sign of new life from the old, of resurrection from the dead? How can we establish a correlation between, on the one hand, something new which we human beings create in the power and with the help of the Spirit of God and, on the other hand, the resurrection and new rule of Christ? If these questions remain unanswered, the statements of our Faith and Order studies also remain trite and hackneyed. Another urgent requirement is a thorough discussion between the Marxist vision of the "new humanity" and the *kainos anthropos* of the New Testament. It is impossible to keep the resurrection of Jesus and the establishment of the rule of God as confessed in the ancient church Creed in some separate self-contained history hovering above the realities of our world and life. On that point, all the participants in the consultations were in basic agreement, yet the texts they have produced reflect this insight only vaguely and very imperfectly.

5. Open fronts in spite of dogmatic sterility

At all events, I came away from the Stavanger Faith and Order Conference with the firm impression that, in spite of the dogmatic sterility once again evident in the case of almost all the representatives of the different denominations, the fronts, i.e. the real questions, still remained open. That is a good sign and a real stimulus to continued ecumenical effort. What seems to me much less encouraging is the way things have developed since Stavanger. In the D and E texts I find a suggestion that more questions had been tidied up and settled than can legitimately be the case after the experience in Stavanger. Dogmatic sterility is more to be feared than open fronts. By "sterility" I mean the readiness to arrange formulas recognized as correct in such a way as to display as few open fronts as possible. The effort to do this seems to me not to qualify as ecumenically responsible. We cannot be content, of course, merely to identify fronts and to list the main questions. But every theological answer we try to provide should at the same time presuppose as such the freedom both to pose fresh questions and, in relation to other confessional traditions which are unfamiliar to us, to recognize and accept as valid new insights and even new tasks.

Concluding remarks

1. The movement from the spontaneous to the dogmatic

It is not to be taken as a complaint if, in conclusion and to sum up, I register my impression that, on our way from preparatory studies over many years down to the beginning of our Faith and Order project in Kottayam and on to the final version of the texts in Berlin/Potsdam, the trend has been away from the spontaneous to the dogmatic. This reflects a movement typical of church history generally: a movement of consolidation and bifurcation or ramification, of explanation and clarification or intellectualization, which, while perfectly intelligible in itself, is nevertheless open to criticism. It would be most regrettable if the continuation of our project were to be characterized by a permanent hardening in this sense. Little good could then be forthcoming from the final product of our labours. For whom are our texts really intended? Are we yet sufficiently clear on this point? Are we to address the teachers of our churches? In that case, a precise and unambiguous type of language would be appropriate. Or are we to address the ministers, pastors and catechists, a much wider audience? Once again we have to use a different style of language. These questions need clearing up, it seems to me.

2. Handling exegetical problems

It seems to me that, in the draft texts so far, from A to E, the use of biblical references is characterized by the stringing together of biblical passages. There are very few passages which are really analyzed exegetically. In most cases it is assumed that their interpretation is more or less clear. But in many instances, this is simply not the case. Possible ways of treating the biblical reference would be: the quotation of scholarly works, the listing of variant interpretations of vital biblical texts, or, again, the attempt to provide an actual brief interpretation of passages cited. The procedure adopted so far, however, seems to me on the whole questionable. No one, surely, is going to deny that only in rare cases is it theologically defensible simply to list biblical references.

3. Structural problems in Faith and Order

Without wishing to make any radical criticism, I would like to register my disquiet at the fact that texts which have been produced in consultations lasting more than a week each have subsequently been completely revised by small committees in which theologians who themselves for the most part were not members of the said consultations have played an active role. I have doubts as to the advisability or wisdom of continuing to employ this method in the future. Of course, every theologian can correct, criticize and improve things in any text, can supplement it and in every case be able to give reasonable grounds for proceeding in this way. But is there still any real continuity if jointly produced texts are revised, shortened and expanded by others at a later date? In this connection, mention should also be made of the problem which arises from the separation between the elected members of the Faith and Order Plenary Commission and the Standing Commission. If the authority to decide rests ultimately with the members of the Standing Commission, can the Faith and Order Plenary Commission be anything more than a "sounding board"? There could be no objection to this if the members of the Plenary Commission had not been chosen as such by their churches. If they were appointed simply as supplementary commentators, that would put a different complexion on things. The development of the texts we have discussed here from Kottayam to Potsdam illustrates perfectly the structural difficulties attending the whole work of the Faith and Order Commission.

4. The way ahead . . . ?

It seems unlikely to me that the E text (Berlin/Potsdam) has any real future as a preliminary draft for the "common expression of the apostolic faith" we seek. Certainly it is possible that it will be accepted by theologians of the different denominations, but I do not believe that it can constitute the basis for the document we want to produce. The Faith and Order project of a common confession of the apostolic faith by the representatives of all the churches together is, I believe, historically unique, and we should do our utmost to carry this project to a conclusion in a responsible way. It may be that the texts so far produced can serve as preliminary studies on the way to the achievement of a text, rich in content and consensus building, a text in which all the churches can recognize themselves and their faith.

PART III

The Third Article

We Believe in the Holy Spirit, the Church and the Life of the World to Come

An Ecumenical Explication

Report of a Faith and Order Consultation
held at Chantilly, France, 3–10 January 1985

A. The Holy Spirit

    I. Belief in the Holy Spirit

    II. The Lord

    III. Giver of Life

    IV. Procession from the Father

    V. Worship and glorification

    VI. The Spirit and the prophets

B. The one, holy, catholic and apostolic church

    I. The church, local and universal community

    II. The church in Trinitarian perspective

        a) The church, people of God

        b) The church, body of Christ

        c) The church, communion of saints in the Spirit

    III. The church as eucharistic, transforming and eschatological community

    IV. The one, holy, catholic and apostolic church

C. The resurrection of the body and the life of the world to come

    I. The church as a community of hope

    II. Jesus Christ — the hope of the world

    III. The oneness and wholeness of Christian hope

        a) Kingdom of God

        b) Resurrection

        c) New heaven and earth

    IV. Living out our hope

A. THE HOLY SPIRIT

1. Faith in the Holy Spirit always belongs with faith in God and in Jesus Christ. To believe "in one God the Father Almighty" and "in one Lord Jesus Christ, the only-begotten Son of God . . ." is to believe also "in the Holy Spirit, the Lord and Life-giver". The Holy Spirit is never experienced, confessed or conceived of apart from the *one* God and his Son and word, whose Spirit he is. In turn, it is through the Spirit that we believe in the Father and the Son. He it is who gives us knowledge of God and his will for us (John 16:12–15; 1 Cor. 2:10–16).

2. Faith in the Holy Spirit also always includes the church of God and of Christ, the confession of one baptism for the remission of sins, and the expectation of the resurrection of the dead and the life of the age to come whose very content as the kingdom of God in Christ is "righteousness and peace and joy in the Holy Spirit" (Rom. 14:17).

God, whose eternal plan is to unite all things in heaven and on earth in Christ, has made his Son "the head over all things for the church which is his body, the fullness of him who wills all in all" — in the Spirit (cf. Eph. 1:22f.).

Through his mighty acts of creation, redemption and sanctification by his Son and Spirit, God fills all things with himself and fully opens his divine being and life to all creatures to become "partakers of the divine nature" (2 Pet. 1:4; cf. Eph. 4:10). In this way believers enter into *communion* with the Triune God. For this reason the saints have testified that where the Holy Spirit is, there is the church and every grace of God in Christ; that where the Holy Spirit is, there is God's kingdom which is fullness of life in Jesus Christ the King.

I. Belief in the Holy Spirit

3. Belief in the Holy Spirit is an act of *confession* which witnesses to a living experience ever to be renewed. It is testimony to the conviction that God's own Spirit is present in the world, living and acting in the community of believers who confess Jesus as "Lord", and cry "Abba" to the most high God, and who, thereby, receive the Spirit's varied gifts, including the charism of discerning spirits inside and outside the church, "to see whether they are from God" (1 John 4:1ff.).

> *Commentary*: Christians differ in their understanding concerning the activity of the Holy Spirit outside the church. While some would claim that "whatever is true, whatever is honourable, whatever is just" (Phil. 4:8) in the life and actions of non-Christians and even unbelievers is of God's Holy Spirit, others say that the sovereignty of the Spirit in history and in people who are unfamiliar with the gospel is hidden from our eyes and can neither be identified nor interpreted in any specific way. In any case, all agree that "there is no other name under heaven . . . by which we may receive salvation" (Acts 4:12) than that of Jesus Christ.

God's spirit is *holy* with the wondrous holiness of the God whose innermost being and life is incomparable to anything in creation. Yet in the Holy Spirit whom God pours out on all flesh through Jesus "the Holy One of God" (Mark 1:24) who is revealed as Christ and Lord through what he suffers, creatures can actually fulfill the commandment of God who says: "You shall be holy, for I am holy" (Lev. 11:44–45; 1 Pet. 1:16). To share God's holiness, without which no person can find life and salvation, is a gracious gift concretely realized in different ways: through active work for goodness, justice and peace as well as through patience, endurance and suffering.

4. The Holy *Spirit* is God's very breath; the living and life-creating power, truth and love of his divine person perfectly imaged in his only-begotten Son. God's Spirit is not one of the many spirits which inhabit the universe. Nor is God's Spirit called "spirit" in contrast to "matter". God's Spirit is not only opposed to all sorts of occult spiritualism, but to every form of material and spiritual evil.

The Holy Spirit of God reveals the spiritual dimension of everything material as he is concretely present in every element of creation, in people's bodies and spirits and souls (cf. Ps. 139:7–10; 1 Thess. 5:23). Through the Holy Spirit all matter is sanctified by God's grace, while apart from him all spiritual things become carnal and dead.

II. The Lord

5. The Holy Spirit is the *Lord.* Being a divine person, he takes his place with God the Lord (*Theos Kyrios*) and Christ the Lord (*Christos Kyrios*).

In confessing the Spirit as Lord (the septuagint translation of *YHWH*, the divine name), the church acclaims his divinity, the same divinity as that of the Father and the Son, and acknowledges his lordship over all creation and history.

> *Commentary*: The Creed does not call the Holy Spirit "God" as it does the Son when it refers to him as "true God of true God". Neither does the Creed use the term *homoousios* to describe the identity of divinity between the Holy Spirit and God the Father, and so of the Son, as later theology does. Some reasons for this, which are of course open to further study and debate, are the desire to employ scriptural words; to avoid confusion of the Holy Spirit with the Son of God through the use of the same terms; and to make it easier for the Creed to be understood and accepted in the churches. In using the title "Lord" for the Holy Spirit, however, the Creed affirms that the Spirit's divinity is exactly that of the Father and the Son which was defended through the use of the term *homoousios*. Thereby the church establishes its doctrine of the Holy Trinity of three divine persons (or *hypostases*) — Father, Son and Holy Spirit — in the perfect unity of one and the same divine being (*ousia*).

The Spirit's lordship is that of divine magnificence and glory which inspires admiration, adoration and obedience from all who receive him. It is not a lordship of brute force, oppressive power or tyrannous manipulation. It is on the contrary a lordship which frees all creation and grants "the glorious liberty of the children of God" (cf. Rom. 8:21). Evil spirits possess. Spiritless flesh enslaves. Wicked powers oppress, dominate, manipulate and exploit. The Spirit of God and Christ liberates people, even in the most oppressive and enslaving of human conditions; and empowers them to resist the evil and to work to overcome it. For "the Lord is the Spirit, and where the Spirit of the Lord is, there is freedom" (2 Cor. 3:17).

III. The Giver of Life

6. The Holy Spirit is the "Giver of Life". He comes forth from the Father as the "life-creator" (*zoopoion*). Without him nothing would be alive (cf. Gen. 1:2). Humankind itself, all living creatures and the living earth at the heart of all that exists are *alive* because of the Spirit of God. So it is that Christians reverence all life, especially all human life; and they resist all that brings death or diminishes the value of any human being. In turn they respect the life of all living creatures, the

animals, the birds of the air, and fish of the sea on which they depend for their very survival; and they resist destruction and abuse of the earth, its rivers and seas and the skies above it. Life always remains a *gift* of God. As he has given his Spirit, he alone can take it away (cf. Ps. 104:29–30).

The Spirit also creates, brings to birth, the *new* life of Christ. Because he is given, human beings are born anew, recreated; and the whole order of existence is transformed into the first fruits of the new creation, the beginnings of the new heaven and the new earth (cf. Rom. 8:11; 2 Cor. 5:17). Through the gift of the Spirit baptism becomes the ever-fertile womb of a Spirit-enlivened church, the *living* body of Christ. Like a mother the Spirit brings to birth new children of the Father, in the one Son whose own humanity he has already filled with life.

> *Commentary*: While agreeing on the *motherly* actions of the Holy Spirit, Christians disagree as to how this feminine image is to be further developed. Because God's Spirit (*Ru'ah*) is feminine in Hebrew and related languages, some contend that the Holy Spirit must be considered somehow as a "feminine principle" in God, and be referred to as "she". Others, however, affirm the scriptural imagery with the symbolic analogy and the use of metaphorical language, while retaining the masculine gender "he" as traditionally used. The common usage of the languages of Commission members presently determines the gender employed when references are made to the Holy Spirit in Faith and Order documents.

The Spirit's gift of life, the life of Christ himself, enables Christians to truly live together as the one body of Christ, and to be bearers of life, Christ-bearers, to all people. So it is that Christians seek to nourish this life through the word and the eucharist, and through the service of others, through which the Spirit fills them ever anew. And in turn they need to struggle against everything which inhibits the free flow of this life into themselves and its manifestation within the church and in the world.

Just as the life-giving Spirit provided manifold gifts for his people Israel, so he also pours out an abundance of charisma for the building-up of the church and for service in the world, such as teaching, prophecy, healing, miracles, tongues and the discernment of spirit (cf. 1 Cor. 12:4–11, 27–30).

IV. Procession from the Father

7. The Holy Spirit "proceeds from the Father". He is breathed forth by the Father. He is the life-giving breath, the Spirit of God. The Father is also the Father of the Son and so the Spirit who is breathed forth is always in relation to the Son, and is so even in the breathing forth.

Western Christians have used the phrase *filioque* to express this latter relation. Eastern Christians have found most interpretations of its meaning unacceptable and so have stressed that the Spirit proceeds from the Father alone. Both have wished to be faithful to the affirmation of the Nicene-Constantinopolitan Creed that the Spirit proceeds from the Father. On that affirmation all Christians can agree.

> *Commentary*: Because East and West are so different, Eastern and Western Christians have come to express the one faith they share, even their understanding of the one original Creed they share, in differing ways. On the foundation of this common faith they must find a way to explain these

different understandings to each other that is both faithful to their orginal common confession, and is scrupulous in its concern to demand nothing of the other which would be for them a betrayal of their vision of the original common faith. This process of explaining and learning from each other will take time but it has begun (e.g. Klingenthal, France, 1978–79[1]; Riva del Garda, Italy, 1984[2]). It has to be possible because the same Holy Spirit who "proceeds from the Father" gives life to the faith of Christians in both the East and the West. As they, through his life-giving power, proceed on this path of mutual understanding they should confess together and in their own churches the Creed as their forefathers did, in the original form.

The issue of the *procession* of the Holy Spirit is relevant even for those Christians who have never placed much importance on the Creeds of the early church. Without a profound understanding of the relation between the Father, the Son and the Holy Spirit, Christians might be forced to endure again the crises which led the early church to formulate the Creed in the first place. These may not take the same form as the early debates but because the Trinity is at the heart of the church's life crises inevitably arise, e.g. about the work of the Holy Spirit in the community, which can only be avoided or resolved through a common profession of the one Trinitarian faith with all its consequences for the life of the church.

V. Worship and glorification

8. The Holy Spirit of God "together with the Father and the Son, is worshipped and glorified". He is the Lord. So it is that the most basic Christian prayer is glory and praise of the Triune God. So it is that *spirituality* is only fully and maturely Christian when it is Trinitarian. So it is that Christians in their daily life and especially in their worship pray that the Father send his Spirit that they might be more completely conformed to the life of Christ the Son (cf. Rom. 8:29). In turn they reject any claims about the activity of the Holy Spirit in the lives of individuals or communities which would have him acting independently of the Father or the Son. Furthermore churches which have not placed much emphasis on Trinitarian spirituality, or prayed for the gift and action of the Holy Spirit (*epiklesis*), are now rediscovering this deepest dimension of Christian life and worship. Christians, therefore, glorify the Triune God through prayer, common worship and the daily service which is their acceptable sacrifice (cf. Rom. 12:1).

VI. The Spirit and the prophets

9. The Holy Spirit "has spoken through the prophets". In this affirmation the church insists that God's Spirit who anointed Jesus and is given to his disciples is the same Spirit who anointed the *prophets of Israel* and inspired the canonical Hebrew scriptures. The Jewish people have not ceased through the centuries to listen and respond to God's Spirit speaking through these scriptures. Christians likewise, continue to be confronted by the Spirit through the prophets. In this, hope is given that the Spirit of God will draw both communities together by his continuing activity (Rom. 11:29–32).

> *Commentary*: When the *church fathers* confessed that the Holy Spirit "spoke through the prophets", they thereby rejected any schools of thought among Christians which would deny that the God of the prophets is the same God as the Father of Jesus Christ.

In *our time* many Christians have been led to reconsider the traditional attitude of the church towards the people of Jewish faith. It is recognized that the Hebrew prophets announced an eschatological coming of the Messiah who above all would renew the face of the earth. In view of this proclamation the Messiahship of Jesus may be understood as the beginning of its full realization, and Christians and Jews might be able to come nearer to each other by studying their common expectation of the eschatological Messiah, as prophesied to both Jews and Christians.

10. Christians believe that Jesus is the fulfilment of Old Testament prophecy and is himself God's anointed prophet upon whom the Holy Spirit rested in a definitive way (cf. Acts 3:22–23).

Breathing upon his disciples and giving them the Holy Spirit, Jesus transmitted to his church the power of prophecy (cf. Rom. 12:6). Every gift which he gives, prophecy or movement of renewal he inspires, is related to what God has done in his Spirit-filled Christ.

Christians still receive *prophetic gifts* today. Churches must remain open to these gifts which are expressed in manifold ways, such as in those who proclaim a specific word of God in situations of oppression and injustice as well as in those who by the charismatic gift of the Spirit edify the church in its worship and service. The suffering of prophetic witnesses will always be part of the church's life and service to the world. "The blood of the martyrs is the seed of the church." Those who by the power of the Holy Spirit remain "faithful unto death" will receive "the crown of life" (Rev. 2:11).

Not everyone who claims prophetic gifts, however, is necessarily inspired by the Holy Spirit. The gift of discernment remains to be exercised by believers since "the spirits of prophets are subject to prophets" (1 Cor. 14:32; cf. also 14:22).

> *Commentary*: In the *history of the church* different forms of prophecy occurred. In the New Testament scriptures references are made to prophets and prophetesses (1 Cor. 12:28–29; Acts 15:32, 21:9–10). Later history tells of wondering prophets (Didache), and of prophecy in congregations (Hermas, Irenaeus, a.o.). It was probably the Montanist crisis (2nd century) which dealt a heavy blow to charismatic prophecy in the church which for the fathers who wrote the Creed was no longer a living reality. After this time prophecy was largely a marginalized, though often recurring phenomenon in church history unitl the twentieth century, when it has become strongly advocated by apostolic and pentecostal churches on the one hand, and the charismatic renewal movements in traditional churches on the other.

B. THE ONE HOLY, CATHOLIC AND APOSTOLIC CHURCH

I. The church, local and universal community

1. The church is the community, local and universal, of those people who adhere to Christ by faith, are baptized for the forgiveness of sins, desire to persevere in a life nourished by the word of God and the sacraments, and are consecrated to the witness and service of the gospel in a communion of love.

The church has its *origin* in the Trinity. It is "the people united by the unity of the Father and the Son and the Holy Spirit".[3] The Father wills it as the people of his possession; the Son consecrates it as his living body; the Spirit gathers it into a unique communion.

The church was founded by Christ, the word of God. It was built on the foundation of the apostles and prophets, Jesus Christ being himself the corner-stone (Eph. 2:20). It was made manifest in the Lord's Supper (Luke 22:7-20), on the cross (John 19:25-35), in the resurrection (John 20:19-23) and at Pentecost (Acts 2:1-4). It shares and continues the work of Christ on earth. It is the creation and the vehicle of the Holy Spirit in the world.

> *Commentary*: We have discovered that we sometimes have difficulties in receiving each other's statements about the church simply because we use *the word "church"* differently.
>
> In the *Eastern* Christian tradition this concept is so predominantly linked with the theological mystery of being-the-church that the perfection of the church, known only by faith, dominates the orientation and renders it practically meaningless to speak of a church sinful, imperfect, in need of change etc. To voice the generally accepted conviction that the individual Christians of whom the church is composed are people who claim no perfection of their own, then demands a language which permits no stain to fall on the church as "church".
>
> In the *Western* churches it is more common to link statements of faith and statements of observation — the church as theological mystery, and the church as sociological event — in a dialectical language of saint-and-sinner, thus expressing the tension of faith and observation in one unified conceptuality.
>
> This difference of language certainly implies less of substantial theological disagreement than it immediately seems to, but does it at the same time indicate some wide-ranging difference in the basic direction of ecclesiological orientation?

II. The church in Trinitarian perspective

a) The church, people of God

2. Throughout scripture, God chooses a *special people* to serve with and for God to the benefit of all peoples. Precisely this is the vocation given to the church in Jesus Christ. In bringing the world the glad tidings of salvation in Jesus Christ, the church does not isolate itself from its environment. Rather, in its particularity, it serves God in solidarity with the whole of humankind.

The New Testament takes up and elaborates the Old Testament concept of a "chosen generation, a royal priesthood, a holy nation, a peculiar people", in applying it to the church and its calling to "show forth the praises of him who has called it out of darkness into his marvellous light" (1 Pet. 2:5, 9; cf Ex. 19:6), linking thus the *ekklesia* of the new covenant with its forerunner and model the *kahal* of the old. Both are chosen to serve in their turn as agents of God's will for humankind as a whole.

Through baptism and faith people are incorporated into the church as God's people. At the same time it should be borne in mind that only the Last Day, which makes all hidden things visible, will make clear who did really belong to the people of God and who did not. The borders of the church are finally known only to God.

b) The church, body of Christ

3. Each of the several images in which the New Testament speaks of the church (God's people, building, vine, etc.) has its own importance, but particular attention has in the tradition been given to that of the *body of Christ* (Rom. 12:4f.; 1 Cor. 12:12–27; Eph. 1:22f.). This image underscores the intimate organic relationship between the living Lord and all those receiving their living hope from him, and also the integral unity of the community of believers, such as it is constituted in and by him. At the same time it underscores the basic importance of his incarnation, passion and resurrection (his bodiliness) for the salvation of the world and recalls the constitutive role of eucharistic presence (his body and blood) in Christian life. The very fruit of salvation: *koinonia* renewed and re-established between God and humankind, between human persons and between humans and the world of creation, is brought about, and is manifested, by the holy mystery of the body of Christ.

The church as Christ's living body is local and universal, particular and inclusive. Called to serve the Lord through the diversity of its members, the church embodies God's creative word as vehicle of his very presence. The royal priesthood of all the faithful and the diverse ordained ministries are serving God in the body of Christ by the power of the Holy Spirit. It thus reflects the active presence of the Trinity in the world, and the event of the incarnation as the event opening up this presence in its essential salutary importance.

c) The church, communion of saints in the Spirit

4. The church as the *koinonia* of saints unites the faithful of every age and of all places in one fellowship of prayer, praise, and sharing of suffering and joy. In the New Testament as well as in the Old Testament the Spirit of God is particularly underscored as God's creative power, bringing forth new life, in the world but also in the community of worship and adoration. The work of the Spirit is intimately connected with divine promise and thus with the word of God and with the guidance given by this word to God's people. The Spirit brings forth God's congregation and equips its members for their service of thanksgiving and praise. At the same time the Spirit acts with divine freedom, and does not restrict divine, renewing creation to events expected or foreseen by God's people.

All ages, including our own, contribute to the hosts of witnesses and martyrs who in their sufferings "complete what is lacking in Christ's afflictions for the sake of his body, that is, the church" (Col. 1:24). Their suffering with and for the church obliges the church in its totality to participation with them in concern and in intercession.

> *Commentary:* The concept of the Apostolic Creed *"communio sanctorum"* can be understood and has been understood in different ways. "Sanctorum" can be either neutrum or masculinum. The meanings would then be, respectively: "a communion sustained by holy gifts", or: "a communion consisting of holy persons". The former would obviously refer to the divine word and to the holy sacraments (including — eventually — certain regulations necessary to secure their operation). Both meanings may be not only historically justifiable, but — in the full context of Christian faith — simply necessary. That in the course of time some churches have been more inclined to underline the first, others more the second aspect may partly be seen as legitimate expressions of mutually complementary vocations.

As to the sanctity of persons, there has been a different stress laid on, respectively holiness as a corporate quality in which all Christians share by faith in Christ, and on holiness as the fruit of sanctification, obtained to a different degree by different Christians. It has generally been seen as being of decisive importance, on the one side, that no Christian should put hope or confidence in the degree of observable holiness obtained by him- or herself, on the other side, that no one should be excused from pursuing sanctification by the general givenness of sanctity in the wider Christian fellowship. The designation of certain Christians as "saints", and the conscious integration of sainthood in Christian worship in "catholic" traditions, have during the centuries been important topics of ecumenical controversy. There seems today to be widespread agreement between the traditions that even if much of the historical criticism of misunderstandings and abuse frequently connected with the worship of saints was justified and necessary, a way needs to be found for the whole oikoumene to jointly explore and reconquer the inclusivity of the mystery of Christ such as it is basically reflected in the authentic concept and in the genuine liturgical inclusion of the "saints".

III. The church as eucharistic, transforming and eschatological community

5. The church is the *eucharistic community* — receiving, sharing and thanksgiving — the basic calling of which is to worship the Triune God. In listening to the word of God and in celebrating the sacraments according to Christ's institution, it is called to offer the prayer, praise and worship of Christians, not only on behalf of themselves, but on behalf of all humankind and of the whole of creation.

This eucharistic vision of being-the-church unites the universality of creation with the uniqueness of incarnation in the permanent actuality of sacramental presence (the body of Christ given *for* and given *to* humankind/the church representing humankind to the body of Christ). At the same time it opens up for a comprehensive understanding of the ultimate relatedness of all authentic creational aspirations, and thus for the unity of "spiritual" and "material" service, of *"leitourgia"* and *"diakonia"*. The worshipping community is at the same time contemplative and active, being served and serving, receiving and giving, and will so remain until the end of times, when it is consumed by the all-comprehending and all-restoring kingdom of God.

6. The church is the *testimony of God's active and transforming presence* in the world. As the vehicle of the word of God on earth it does not exist for itself, but for the world. It is not a fortress in which people can enclose themselves for a life in security, but a servant people spread throughout the world, sent not only to sow the good seed of the word, but also to look after the seed which Christ, the universal Lord, has already sown abundantly all over the earth — working and praying for this seed to grow by the radiance of the light of the Holy Spirit. It rejoices in all the signs of the caring work of the Creator which it encounters in the world, all truth, all beauty and all goodness. It encourages the growth of these human values, fruits of the hidden action of God, in the hope to bring them to the final matureness in the kingdom by the light of the gospel and the nourishment of the sacraments. It is the total richness of creation which the church offers to the praise of God in the thanksgiving of the eucharist, in order for it to be restored in the full transfiguration of the Creator's "new creation".

7. The church is the *prefiguration of the kingdom* which it expects and announces. As such it is called to a life in sanctifying transformation. At the same

time as it is conscious of being here on earth a communion of sinful beings, it is aware of its true identity as a reality transcending all merely sensible observation. It cannot be subject to the realities of this world, as it is oriented towards the coming kingdom which it proclaims in word and deed. It awaits the glorious return of Christ, its Lord, an expectancy which it expresses most vigorously in its liturgy. The church can have no other attitude towards human power and wealth than that of detachment and freedom. The church as a servant church is a poor and powerless church, totally dependent upon its Master, who alone can turn its poverty into the final fullness of perfection.

IV. The one, holy, catholic and apostolic church

8. There is only one holy church and it is catholic and apostolic in each place by its faithfulness to the word of God, its link with the Lord, Head of the body, and its communion in the Holy Spirit with all the local churches of God irrespective of space and time.

a) There is but *one church* in the diversity of the local churches. All the baptized are incorporated into a single body, called to witness to their one and only Saviour. The unity of all Christians has to show itself visibly in the unity of the fundamental faith and the sacramental life. The one baptism, the one holy scripture, the Creeds of the ancient church and common prayer point towards this visible unity which can be fully accomplished only in one common celebration of the eucharist. This unity does not imply uniformity, but an organic bond of unity between all the local churches in their valid diversities so that all the baptized, confessing the same faith, are able to share together in the same sacraments, in particular the same eucharist, the sign of their unity in the body of Christ (conciliarity — reconciled diversity).

b) The Holy Spirit dwells in the *holy church*. This church has been set apart by God who is holy and who sanctifies it by the good deposit of word and sacraments. It is holy because of the holy words it proclaims and the holy acts it performs, and also a community of sinners, but sinners who have been and who are constantly being forgiven. We must make a distinction in the church between the holy ministry of word and sacraments, and the imperfect persons who exercise that holy ministry. The holiness of the church signifies the faithfulness of God towards his people: the gates of hell will not prevail against it. Even at the darkest times in the church's history, Christ preserves the essence of its being and service for the salvation of humankind.

c) Christ, full of grace and truth, is already present on earth in the *church catholic*. It is only in the whole (*katholikè*) that the local church finds its true identity, the fullness of truth and of judgment. The being of the church in its fullness is gathered and expressed in great diversity through the Christian spiritual life of all peoples in space and time. This fullness of the universal church limits nationalism and particular traditions to their proper perspective. The fullness of the universal church is a fullness of life; in the life of the church the whole human being is enlisted for the worship and the service of God; this fullness can be seen in Christian liturgy as well as in Christian daily life, both of which demand the participation of our entire being and the whole creation to the glory of God. "Where Jesus Christ is, there too is the Church catholic."[4] Where Jesus Christ is, there the church is present through the power of the Spirit as the fullness of truth and salvation, and there, in all ages, it makes people participants of his life and salvation, irrespective of sex, race or position.

d) The church is apostolic:
—in that it recognizes its fundamental identity with the church of Christ's apostles, as presented in the New Testament;
—in its faithfulness to the word of God lived out and understood in the apostolic Tradition, guided by the Holy Spirit throughout the centuries, and expressed in the Creeds;
—by its celebration of the sacraments instituted by Christ and practised by the apostles;
—by the continuity of its ministry, initially taken up by the apostles, in the service of Christ;
—being a missionary church which, following the example of the apostles, will not cease to proclaim the gospel to the whole of humankind until Christ comes again in glory.

    Commentary: (A commentary on apostolic succession is to be drafted, see "Baptism, Eucharist and Ministry".)

C. THE RESURRECTION OF THE BODY AND THE LIFE OF THE WORLD TO COME

I. The church as a community of hope

1. The church is a *"communion of hope"* (Bangalore 1978[5]) in the midst of a world that sees death and catastrophe in its future. This hope is not arbitrary, because the church participates now in the future God has prepared for all creatures. In the church the reign of Christ is present in the world. Thus, it is a sign of God's future for the renewal of humanity. The church also looks forward to the final kingdom that is yet to come. It looks for its own and the world's fulfilment (cf. Edinburgh, 1937).[6] The church awaits the fulfilment of the reality of reconciliation already at the centre of its life through the Spirit. The church's hope is foremost, however, a hope for the world and a trust in God's redemptive promise of faithfulness to his entire creation. (By "the world" is here meant the entirety of God's creation, both within and beyond the community gathered around the word and sacraments.)

II. Jesus Christ — the hope of the world

2. In Jesus Christ, his life and work, death and resurrection, God manifests the future he intends for the world through the Spirit. As first-born from the dead, Jesus is the realization and manifestation of the *new* humanity. In Jesus, life eternal enters our lives, lifting them out of death and into communion with God. The Spirit poured out by the Risen Christ is the seal of our hope. Our hope is a hope for what is beyond human capacities and expectations (Heb. 11:1), a hope against hope. Yet, it is a confident hope, because it rests on the powerful promise of God.

III. The oneness and wholeness of Christian hope

3. The church has *one* hope; "there is one body and one Spirit, just as you were called to the one hope that belongs to your call" (Eph. 4:4). This *one* Christian hope is expressed in the biblical witness to the kingdom of God, the resurrection, and the new heaven and earth. These aspects of our hope are inseparably intertwined, yet can be distinguished in order to affirm Christian hope in its social, individual and cosmic dimensions.

a) Kingdom of God

4. The kingdom of God is the *sovereign* reign of God through his Son Jesus Christ in the Spirit. Under God's sovereign reign, the forces of evil, sin, and death, the principalities and powers of the age (1 Cor. 15:24f.; Col. 2:15) are overcome through the cross and resurrection (Phil 2:5–11). Our sins are forgiven and we are freed from fear of the forces of evil. While the sovereign reign of God is a lordship of power, it is the reign of the cross. The sovereignty of the kingdom is manifest in the lowly service of Jesus and is not a lordship of domination. The Kingdom of God is the fulfilment of the prophecy to Israel (Isa. 11:1–11; Micah 4:3) of the establishment of justice, righteousness and peace, God's will done on earth as in heaven. This kingdom is the *koinonia* of humanity, the consummation of the communion of the saints. In this koinonia, all nations will come to the feast of the Lamb.

b) Resurrection

5. The forces of death are present throughout life. *Death* invades and destroys life and seeks to separate us from our brothers and sisters and from God. Death is conquered in the cross and resurrection of Christ. In baptism (Rom. 6:3ff.) and throughout the Christian life, we participate in Christ's death and resurrection and receive his life-giving Spirit. We rise into the fullness of life God promises to his creatures.

6. The focus of our hope for life with God beyond death according to the New Testament (1 Thess. 4:13–18; Matt. 25:31ff.; 1 Cor. 15:3ff.) and the Creed is the *resurrection of the dead*. We also affirm that those who have died with Christ now live in Christ.

> *Commentary*: The *status of the dead* between death and the final resurrection has been understood in various ways. The idea of the immortality of the soul, important for much of Christian history, has been both affirmed and denied in recent years. Different beliefs about the status of the dead and their relation to the living lead to divergent beliefs and practices in relation to prayers for the dead, prayers by the dead, the invocation of the saints, and a purgational period after death.

7. Resurrection involves an encounter with the living God and his *judgment* of good and evil within personal and communal life. God creates an accountable humanity and will be faithful to his creation; all will be called to account in God's still open judgment. We affirm that it is not the eternal will of God to condemn and destroy the world he has created. In giving his Son he wants his world to be saved through his Son (John 3:17). The universal saving intention of God (1 Tim. 2:4) cannot be the basis of a presumptuous security. The apostolic witness explicitly reckons with an outer darkness and the possibility of being cast into it. Such a possibility will never be based on a lack of God's will to save.

> *Commentary*: While some have defended universal salvation, most Christian thought has assumed that many will be lost to salvation and condemned. *Apocatastasis* or the assured salvation of all creatures has been rejected by official doctrinal statements of all churches except those who are denominationally "universalist". Nevertheless, prominent voices have recently suggested that only the possibility that some will be condemned need be asserted.

The judgment of God is passed through his Son, in unity with his Spirit and his church. "Christ will come as the revelation of truth and righteousness. The ultimate judgment of the world is his, our assurance that the murderer will never ultimately triumph over the victim" (Bangalore[7]). Our judge is our Saviour; we are judged by the God who justifies.

c) New heaven and earth

8. We will rise in our full humanity, not as disembodied spirits. What was sown in perishability will rise imperishable (1 Cor. 15:52). While creation will be transformed in ways that are still a mystery, no essential aspect of creation will be lost. In Christ God sets forth his "plan for the fullness of time, to unite all things in him, things in heaven and things on earth" (Eph. 1:10). Not only heavenly but also earthly things, the wholeness of creation, will find a place in the kingdom of God. The water of baptism and the bread and wine of the eucharist we already see as the inclusion of earthly things in the celebration of God. In the new heaven and new earth (Isa. 65:17; Rev. 21:1), the *communion of creation*, in perfect openness one to another, will praise God face to face (1 Cor. 13:12). Creation will be unified and transformed in the abiding reality of God's love (1 Cor. 13:13). God will be all in all (1 Cor. 15:28).

IV. Living out our hope

9. In our hope we can live with confidence and trust in the promises of God in the midst of a world that seems closed in its future. Because the *final future* is in the sure hands of God, we need not be anxious for tomorrow (Matt. 6:34). We are freed by our hope to work for a more humane and just world. Our faithful pursuit of justice and peace within history cannot bring in the kingdom (see §10), but our work is done "in the trust that nothing of what we have done in expectation of that Holy City will be lost" (Riva del Garda[8]). We are freed to rejoice with those who rejoice and to weep with those who weep. Because our hope is grounded in God, we can take the risk (cf. Bangalore[9]) of opening ourselves to the joys and sufferings of the world.

10. *Affirming* our hope for this world, we deny any escape from this world and its problems, either by losing ourselves in the accumulation of things or by an otherworldly flight away from the neighbour's concrete needs.

— Affirming our trust in the future God has prepared for us, we deny any attempt to secure our future at the expense of the world, especially through the threat of mass destruction.
— Affirming the presence of the yet future kingdom, we deny any understanding of God's coming kingdom which either separates the kingdom from this world and its life or identifies the fullness of the kingdom with any historical reality or any human action, not even any present ecclesiastical structure.
— Affirming God's faithfulness to his entire creation, we deny any impoverishment of our hope which blinds us to the wholeness of God's redemption of society, of individuals, or of all creation.
— Affirming that Jesus with his Spirit and church is God's word by which all is explained and judged, we deny that the powers that seem to rule history will finally determine its meaning and destiny.
— In the face of a secularism which does not look beyond itself to God, our hope, living within this world while looking to the world to come, renews itself through worship, prayer, and liturgy.

11. In the face of despair over the world, our hope *refuses* to acquiesce in things as they are.
— In face of growing hopelessness, our hope will declare no situation or person beyond hope.
— In the face of oppression, our hope affirms that oppression will not remain forever.
— In the face of the use of the language of Christian hope to justify political programmes, our hope affirms that the advent of the kingdom of God is not within our capacity, but remains in the power of God's surprising initiative.
— In the face of unbearable pain, incurable disease, and irreversible handicap, our hope affirms that Christ suffers with all who are hopeless.
— In the face of our failure to live out our hope in the world, our hope affirms that the Spirit opens to us ever new ways of being signs to the world of the coming kingdom.

12. In *God alone* is our trust. All that we have received, we have received from his hand. All that we hope for will come from his blessing. To God be glory from age to age. "He who testifies to these things, says, 'surely I am coming soon'. Amen. Come, Lord Jesus" (Rev. 22:20).

NOTES

1. Cf. "The Filioque Clause in Ecumenical Perspective: Klingenthal Memorandum 1979", in "Apostolic Faith Today: a Handbook for Study", H.-G. Link ed., *Faith and Order Paper No. 124*, Geneva, WCC, 1985, pp.231ff.
2. Cf. "Our Credo — Source of Hope. Declaration by Participants of the Third European Ecumenical Encounter, 1984", in "Apostolic Faith Today", *op. cit.,* pp.188ff.
3. Cyprian, *De Orat. Dom.* 23.
4. Ignatius of Antioch, *Ad Smyrn.* 8,12.
5. Cf. "A Common Account of Hope: Final Document. V: The Church: a Communion of Hope", in "Apostolic Faith Today", *op. cit.,* pp.88f.
6. Cf. "The Church of Christ and the World of God, V. The Church and the Kingdom of God", in *The Second World Conference on Faith and Order*, L. Hodgson ed., London, 1938, pp.232f.
7. In "Apostolic Faith Today", *op. cit.,* p.87.
8. *Ibid.,* p.211.
9. *Ibid.,* "Hope as the Invitation to Risk", pp.90ff.

The Prophetic Spirit, the Church as a Community and Living Our Hope

Ecumenical Aspects of the Third Article of the Creed

HANS-GEORG LINK

The third article of the Creed covers a wide range from the Spirit's procession from the Father to the life of the world to come. The "age of the church", from Pentecost to the parousia, is included in this all-embracing perspective. It is this which constitutes the special ecumenical relevance of this article of the Creed. For in it the theme which belongs peculiarly to the oikoumene is under discussion: the one, holy, catholic and apostolic church. Both its foundation then and its form now as the body of Christ are involved. Alongside the "marks of the church" (*notae ecclesiae*) ethical standpoints are also in evidence.

Also related to the third article is the "classical" conflict between Eastern and Western church traditions: the Western addition of the *filioque* clause ("and the Son") on the procession of the Spirit from the Father. Although theologians of both traditions have come considerably closer to each other's position in the last few years,[1] it is still not possible to speak of a theological, liturgical, spiritual or even canonical solution to the filioque problem.

Finally, the third article offers a pointer to the basis, content and aim of Christian hope, and in this age of increasing despair, this is of special importance.

For each main theme I shall select one aspect from the multitude of problems and points of view, to give an outline picture of the road travelled from the initial discussion to the "explication" as it now stands.

I. The Spirit who has spoken through the prophets

1. Approaches

In comparison with the Apostles' Creed, which does no more than mention very briefly the fact of the Holy Spirit, the Nicene Creed[2] has much to say as soon as the Holy Spirit is mentioned. The first item stressed is the lordship, and thus the personal quality, of the Spirit; this nowadays raises the question how the personality of the Spirit as the third Person of the Trinity is to be understood. Next, the Spirit is represented as the giver, or, as it were, the mother, of life; many reflections on the feminine element in the Trinity are today associated with these, and also with Hebraic feminine representations of the Spirit. Stress is laid thirdly on the direct procession of the Spirit from the Father without the mediation of the Son; this is where the East-West conflict in pneumatology reached its sad climax in the debate on the source of the Spirit. The fourth emphasis is on the Spirit's equality of rank, doxologically, with the Father and the Son; this is reflected in liturgical epiklesis of the Spirit and generally in the Trinitarian spirituality of the East, which is at present being rediscovered by many churches in the West.

Finally, the Creed confesses the identity of the Holy Spirit with the Spirit "who spoke through the prophets". This pronouncement of the Nicene Creed is all the more important since for more than fifteen hundred years it remained the sole explicit, positive reference to the Old Testament in a Christian confession till we come to the 1948 declaration of the Dutch Hervormde Kerk (Reformed Church) on the relation of Christians and Jews. Here the reference was to the Christian relation, on the one hand to the prophets, the Old Testament as a whole and the past and present of Judaism, and on the other to the relation to present-day prophetic manifestations in the church. I have chosen this last aspect of the Christian confession of the Holy Spirit because it concerns one of the fields which has ecumenically had least work done on it and is at the same time specially important for our understanding of modern prophetic awakenings in the Christian world.

2. *Jürgen Moltmann's interpretation*

Jürgen Moltmann, a Reformed theologian from Tübingen, gave one of the two addresses on the Holy Spirit. In it he made the following comments on the Spirit, "who has spoken through the prophets":

> According to the self-understanding of the Old Testament prophetical writings, therefore, the prophets proclaim the *word of the Lord* in the Spirit of the Lord and the *Spirit of the Lord* leads them to bear witness to the word of the Lord. It is the same Spirit who speaks to us through Jesus Christ (Luke 4:18ff.), in whom Christ has come to us and whom he sends to us. This is what the Nicene clause affirms. But, conversely, it means that the Spirit in whom Christ came and whom he sends to us, had already spoken through the prophets to *Israel*. And if he has spoken through the prophets to Israel, this cannot be restricted to the "Old Testament" and pre-Christian Israel, but also applies to that *Israel beside the church* which hears the prophets by preserving, believing and taking seriously the words of the prophetical writings. The "Spirit who *has* spoken through the prophets" spoke first to Israel before speaking to Christians in the dawning messianic age. If, however, he first spoke through Israel's prophets to Israel, then he must also continue to speak through the writings of these prophets to Israel beside and outside the Christian church. In this respect Israel beside the churches, Judaism beside Christianity is the *other form of the Holy Spirit* who has spoken through the prophets and continues to speak through them. It is not possible to change the perfect tense of this speech of the Holy Spirit through the prophets of Israel into a pluperfect and say: "who had spoken through the prophets" so as to put back Israel and the prophets into the pre-history of the church and put the church in the place of Israel in God's salvation history. The case is, rather, that the brief statement of the Nicene Creed brings Christianity into the *community of the Holy Spirit* with Judaism and to recognition of the people of God which today listens to the Holy Spirit — the "Lord" — who has spoken through its prophets.

Thus for Moltmann there are three paramount aspects:
1) one and the same Spirit of God spoke out of the mouths of the prophets and of Jesus of Nazareth;
2) the Spirit spoke to Israel through the prophets before Christianity and continues to speak right up to the present to the Israel that hearkens to the prophets, alongside the church;
3) it is therefore not possible for the church to make itself a substitute for Israel; rather, the church is brought by this pronouncement of the Nicene Creed into community with the Jews as another manifestation of the Holy Spirit.

3. *From the Chantilly discussion*

In Chantilly there were five aspects that had a part to play:

a) Frieda Haddad, the *Orthodox* theologian from Beirut, had undertaken to give the follow-up address to Moltmann's. While both addresses had common ground in their reflections on the femininity and Trinitarian personality of the Spirit, there is not a single comment in Frieda Haddad's remarks on the Spirit who spoke through the prophets. This silence of hers is extremely telling, for it brings out something of the different attitude of the Orthodox tradition to Judaism, in contrast to Reformed covenant theology. The differing treatments of the theme seem also to indicate the very different situations of these two Christian theologians: Moltmann is trying as a German theologian living in West Germany to arrive at a new, dependable basis for the relation between the church and Judaism. As an Orthodox Christian, Frieda Haddad shared the experience of the bombardment of

Beirut by Israeli forces in 1983/4; seeing herself and her Muslim neighbours in the role of victims to Israeli acts of aggression she can clearly say nothing, against that background, regarding the Spirit who spoke through Israel's prophets. If today a German theologian has to point to the enduring significance of Judaism for salvation history, it is correspondingly difficult for Christians in the Middle East who are suffering from Israeli occupation to recognize in the Israel of today something of that special salvation history character in relation to the church.

b) What did the *Nicene fathers* have in mind with their credal statement? In Chantilly the stress was placed on two aspects. On the one hand, it was said, they rejected a view of the Spirit, and of Christian existence in the Spirit as something acquired and experienced independently of, or in opposition to, the Old Testament — or at its expense; that is, they rejected Marcion's second century position, which moreover has at various times brought one disaster after another on the Christian church, right up to the attempts in the (German) Third Reich to "dejudaize" the Bible and the Christian faith. On the other hand, the Nicene fathers confessed the identity of the Spirit of God in the prophets of Israel and in Jesus of Nazareth. For them this included recognition of the divine inspiration of the prophetic and all other writings of the Old Testament, and hence the acknowledgment of these as normative for their own preaching and living.

c) In the history of Christianity there were various *forms of prophecy*. The sequence begins with the appearance of John the Baptist as a new, eschatological prophet; and in the New Testament Jesus of Nazareth is likewise seen, in part, as standing in the prophetic tradition. Prophecy is one of the gifts of the Spirit, for which every New Testament community is supposed to strive. In the church's beginnings, there were wandering prophets who went from place to place and expounded the will of God to Christian congregations. Christian prophecy reached its first climax with the charismatic movement of Montanus which developed in the second and third centuries into a full-blown ecclesiastical crisis. The conflict between personal charism and institutionalized ministry was argued out here for the first time on a broad front, and was decided in favour of the authority of the ministry. At Chantilly, attention was specifically focused on the point that prophecy was increasingly ousted from its place in the official church, although at times it again caught public attention, as in the instances of Joachim of Fiore and the left wing of the Reformation. Not till the twentieth century has there been a resurgence in the importance of prophetic movements. Pentecostalist churches have come into being, first and foremost in the third world, and the charismatic movement, with its critical attitude towards institutionalism, can be found in almost every continent and confronts the established churches with difficult problems.

d) This leads us to the question of the *content of prophetic gifts*. Since the days of King Saul there has been a dynamic and even ecstatic element in prophecy as a gift of the Spirit. Critical questionings directed at Israel's worship and social structure and likewise at the church can equally be indicators of a prophetic Spirit. But primarily, it was said at Chantilly, the task of a prophet is to expound authoritatively God's will to God's people in a particular situation. For this reason, greater significance attaches to the prophetic message of which the content is a gift of the Spirit, than to accompanying manifestations, which may range from the charismatic to the ecstatic and are at times overvalued and very liable to misuse for dramatic effect. Justice and peace are undoubtedly among the classical prophetic themes. As regards these elements and other forms in which prophecy manifests itself, discerning the spirits is essential. While the Spirit is not to be quenched, it must also be kept in mind that not every spirit is of God. One of the most important of today's ecumenical tasks is to find criteria for discerning the spirits.

e) Following the catastrophe which befell the Jews during the second world war, a new definition of the relation of *Christians and Jews* is needed; not just as a special German act of reparation but rather as a thorough-going ecumenical task. It ties up both with overdue Christian reflection on the faith's Jewish roots and with the identity of the Spirit of God in Jewish and Christian prophets. One of the questions heatedly debated at Chantilly was whether the activity of the Spirit of God can be perceived only within the Christian church, or also outside it. There was nevertheless a good deal of agreement that one of the best ways of achieving rapprochement between Jews and Christians is to look at the expectation of the coming Messiah which they have in common, in the light of the promises given to both in the Hebrew scriptures.

4. The first draft explication

The first draft worked out at Chantilly for an ecumenical explication on the theme of the Holy Spirit generally follows the themes set forth in the Creed. Under the general heading "The Holy Spirit" paragraphs 9 and 10 discuss the relevant credal statement under the sub-heading "The Spirit and the Prophets"[3]. This initial draft explication groups the viewpoints brought together in the Chantilly discussion in two sections. The contents are thus structured as follows:

I. Theme: The Spirit and the Jewish people (Para. 9 with commentary)

Theses: 1. The same spirit was at work in the prophets of Israel and in Jesus of Nazareth.
2. "Through the centuries" the Jewish people have heard and responded to the Spirit.
3. There is hope that the continuing working of the Spirit will bring Jewish and Christian communities closer to each other.

Commentary: 1. The church fathers rejected the separation of the God of the prophets from the Father of Jesus Christ.
2. The traditional attitude of the church towards the Jewish people is currently being reconsidered.
3. Jews and Christians share the expectation of an eschatological Messiah.

II. Theme: The Spirit and the Christian church (Para. 10 with commentary)

Theses: 1. The Holy Spirit rested on God's anointed prophet Jesus in a definitive way.
2. Jesus transmitted the power of prophecy to his church.
3. Today too Christians receive prophetic gifts and bear prophetic witness.
4. Believers must practise discerning the spirits.

Commentary: 1. In church history there were various forms of prophecy.
2. In the twentieth century the phenomenon of prophecy has appeared in the pentecostalist churches and the charismatic movement.

5. Additions

a) The *Geneva revision* of April 1985 added to the Chantilly explication a whole new section with biblical and historical references which provided the interpretation and exegetical and historical support. As regards the Spirit that spoke through the prophets there were some additions dealing with the experience of the first Christian communities in relation to the working of the Spirit in the Old Covenant:

> 4. The first Christian generation acknowledged that the Spirit who was with Christ during his ministry from baptism on (cf. Matt. 3:16; 4:1; Luke 3:22, 4:1,14; etc.) and who was given by the risen Lord was already at work in the Old Covenant: speaking through the prophets, anointing the kings of the people, inspiring the prayers of the faithful.
>
> 5. It is also clear from the New Testament witness that the same Spirit of God who was calling the people of God into one community was also the one who after the resurrection of Christ made of all the believers the body of Christ, a holy temple, the family of God.
>
> 6. The way in which the first Christian communities understood and proclaimed the event of pentecost shows that for them the Spirit poured out on them was the Spirit of the eschatological times already announced by the prophets of the Old Testament.
>
> 7. While taking up in this way the Old Testament witness to the Spirit of God, the primitive church realized, however, in the light of its faith in Jesus Christ, that the Spirit of Jahwe was not only an impersonal power active in history, but also has personal features. In analogy to their understanding of the word of God (*logos*) as the person of the *logos* made flesh in Jesus Christ, they confessed that the Holy Spirit, together with the Father and the Son, is active as a person in the economy of salvation. (III, A.I)

b) The *Crêt-Bérard draft* of June 1985 expands the explication of the criterion for discerning the spirits with this sentence: "The confession of Jesus Christ, according to the Apostle Paul, serves as a criterion of distinguishing the spirit of God from other prophetic spirits (1 Cor. 12:3)" (III, A.III, 25).

6. *From the Stavanger discussion*

In Stavanger the discussion on the Spirit who spoke through the prophets focused on two aspects: the Christian relation to the Jews and prophetic or charismatic phenomena today.

a) On *Christian-Jewish relations* study group 3 remarks that:

> Originally the claim that the Spirit spoke through the prophets was inserted to combat Marcion, and we need to make reference to contemporary forms of Marcionism. The reference to the prophets allows for comment on the relationship between Christianity and Judaism, but the discussion as it stands is inadequate, since it initially implies a triumphalistic Judaism ("The Jewish people have not ceased . . . to listen and respond to God's Spirit . . . "), and since it also traces the commonality of Christianity and Jews to their shared Messianic expectation. Certainly many Jews would not agree that the prophets "announced an eschatological coming of *the* Messiah" and most of contemporary Judaism does not stress Messianic expectation.

In a personal statement, Mgr *Jorge Mejia* from Argentina, the Vatican official responsible for relations with the Jews, made the following four proposals:

> 1. The Old Testament is inspired by the Spirit in the *same* sense and with the *same* consequences as the New. Therefore, it belongs with equal right to the faith and the worship of the church.
>
> 2. All unfavourable comparisons with the *Jewish religion* should be explicitly rejected as if the Christian faith were the "cult in Spirit" and Judaism "the worship in the flesh" or mere "subservience to the Law". The Spirit of God has not certainly

abandoned the Jewish people, but slowly and mysteriously guides it through its final consummation. In such context, the present renewal relationship should be seen.

3. I would tune down the reference to the *Messiah* here and insist more on the common eschatological hope of the kingdom (with its necessary consequence for the service of humankind and the work for the transformation of the world).

4. The origin of the church in the Jewish *matrix* and therefore the continuity in the plan of God should be mentioned, this being the real theological basis for the new relationship.

b) On *modern manifestations of prophecy*, *Horace Russell*, the Baptist theologian from Jamaica, first made the general point that prophecy also plays an important part in Islam and African religious traditions too, and that within Christianity as a whole the charismatic movements merit greater attention in the discussion on the Holy Spirit. Dr *Yeow Choo Lak* from the Presbyterian church in Singapore then made the following detailed comments on this:

> Both the original text and the report of Group II.3 have not paid sufficient attention to the implications of the numerous *charismatic renewals* taking place all over the world. Because of this, many from our supporting churches deeply involved with charismatic renewals will be forced by us to adopt the I-told-you-so position, viz., we are a bunch of theologians with head knowledge only.
>
> Many of our congregations are asking for help as many of our pastors are "new" to the challenges and implications of charismatic renewals. For example, they are being compelled to re-examine spiritual gifts and how these charismata are being exercised in the congregation. Their seminaries have not prepared them for this task.
>
> There is a dire need for our Faith and Order Commission to address itself to a spiritual phenomenon taking place in many of our congregations. This will, at least indirectly, make our material relevant to those involved in charismatic renewal and useful to pastors looking for help in this area.

It appears that many third-world churches are confronted by charismatic and prophetic movements more directly than in the first and second worlds. In this context the report of the study group demands that "the criteria for distinguishing God's Spirit from other spirits should be set forth more fully" than has so far happened in the explication.

7. On the Berlin/Potsdam explication

a) As regards the relations between *the church and the Jews*, it is now said of the church that it is "in continuity with the people of God in the Old Testament" and is "at the same time the People of God of the New Covenant" (III, A.II, 21). While at this fundamental point there is a fuller reference to the relation between Jews and Christians, the recommendation at the end of the commentary is at the same time more general and more cautious in its wording: "Christians and Jews might be able to come nearer to each other by studying their respective eschatological expectations of God's final kingdom and by seeking ways of common service to humankind in this perspective."

b) The *"charismatic renewal"* is now explicitly mentioned among the gifts of prophecy and thus brought out from its sectarian corner into the broad stream of the gifts of the Spirit (para. 23). At the same time an explanation is added regarding the criteria for discerning the spirits: "In the history of the church additional criteria drawn from the biblical witness and the tradition and confession of the church have been employed as required by specific situations and challenges (cf. for example 1 John 4:2,3)."

Whether what has so far been said is adequate on the important problem of the gifts of the Spirit and the criteria for discerning these from other spirits will have to become evident as the discussion proceeds. At all events it is a great ecumenical step forward that in this explication the church and the Jews have been brought into a positive relation with each other. "The Jewish people have continued through the centuries on the basis of their tradition to listen and respond to God's Spirit speaking through these scriptures" (III, A.II,21). It is to be hoped that this ecumenical insight will contribute in increasing measure to overcoming all forms of Christian anti-Jewish attitudes.

II. Community in the one body of Christ: the church

1. Approaches

The Creed refers to the one, holy, catholic and apostolic church as a creation of the Spirit. As an institution it has no life of its own independent of the working of the Spirit but rather participates in the worldwide creative movement of the Spirit. Consequently the four marks of the church should be understood with ecumenical breadth and not confessional narrowness. Connected with this is the challenge to give expression to the unity of the church over against the fact that it is torn apart into many confessions. In the ecumenical context the holiness of the church does not have as its purpose only the sanctification of its members, but aims even more at the display of signs of renewal and solidarity in a worldwide community. How are we to regain today, especially in Protestantism, the catholic dimension of the church, confronted as we are with many kinds of provincialism, and link that dimension with cultural diversity? Apostolicity presupposes firm links with origins and a credible commitment of the churches in today's world.

To make these four marks of the church effective again in the ecumenical age, a comprehensive ecclesiology is needed. In recent ecumenical discussion the model of the body of Christ has proved particularly helpful in linking together the various positions; it plays a key role in the development of a common ecumenical ecclesiology. Here it must be discovered whether we can develop an ecumenical understanding of a unity which will not become a sterile, monotonous uniformity but will rather be the expression of a live fellowship or community. Here too there has to be an explication of catholicity which avoids the hierarchical dangers of Roman Catholicism and instead of this displays ecumenical breadth in cultural diversity. Finally, the body of Christ as the fundamental model for the church has a sacramental and an ethical dimension too.

2. A Roman Catholic, a Lutheran and a Baptist view

a) The Canadian Dominican *Jean Tillard* gave the main theological address at Chantilly: "God's Church in God's Plan". It has two parts: (1) God's church and God's gospel, (2) communion in the body of Christ. At the beginning of the second part Tillard develops his view of the church as the body of Christ:

> Why are Christians the one single body of Christ? Why is their lack of solidarity, especially when it extends so far as to be displayed at the Lord's table, a lack of discernment of that body (1 Cor. 11:17–34)? Because the bread that is broken is "communion with the body of Christ" (10:16–17). The inner unity of the community comes from the fact that all, which embraces each individual with his or her own unique qualities, are caught up in the one indivisible body of Christ the Lord. The body is not formed by the sum of the individual members; rather, it assumes into itself

their multiplicity, and the Spirit of his Lordship welds them together in *koinonia*. The conjunction of singularity and communion, in which the members retain their individuality and yet at the same time are attentive to and concerned for one another — the function which saves them — takes place within the embrace of the body "of peace", "of unity", "of reconciliation", "of charity".

The letter to the Ephesians, which was probably written within the context of intra-ecclesiastical tensions, is the key document with regard to this unitive function of the body of Christ. It places at the heart of its meditation on the church, whose Head is Christ, the Ruler of the whole universe (Eph. 1:20–23), the declaration that hatred, division, separation and alienation have been destroyed, slain, reduced to nothing by the blood of the cross: "You who once were far off have been brought near in the blood of Christ . . . What was divided he has brought into unity: in his flesh he has destroyed the wall of separation, the hatred . . . His desire was to reconcile Jews and Gentiles in one body by means of the cross: there he killed hatred" (2:13–16). The crucified body of Jesus, his "body of flesh" (Col. 1:26; cf. 2:11), perishable and mortal, becomes the place of reconciliation (Col. 1:22) because forgiveness has been obtained through the bloodshed and murder of the cross (Eph. 1:7). The imprint and burden of salvation are revealed on this body given up to death for the sake of the accomplishment of God's gracious plan (the "mystery"), which had as its aim the reunification of the entire universe.

Therefore, Christ's own personal body, in which the drama of pardon and reconciliation were lived out, is in truth the "meeting-point" of the new humanity, the specific place where *koinonia* (described by Paul as a body) becomes constituted and present, already complete in its very essence. In an admirable word which provides a concrete expression of the nature of this "mystery", the blocs or factions of broken humanity here and now find themselves "concorporated" (the *sunsôma* of Eph. 3:6). Thus the resurrection of this body of flesh in a body of glory seals, in the power of the Spirit, the "recapitulation" or "return to unity" of all of humanity in Christ (1:10). The ecclesial body springs to life *in* and *with* the risen body of the Lord (2:6), who is its head in the twofold sense of source of life (as in the medical theory of Hippocrates) and of chief. Thus, held fast in him, the ecclesial body appears as the fullness of Christ (1:23), "that without which Christ would not be complete, but with which he is complete" (J. A. Robinson). In the sense expressed by Paul in his letters to the Corinthians and to the Romans, the body exists only *in* the body of the crucified One who has been glorified by the Spirit. The two cannot be separated. Yet this inclusion of the ecclesial body in the risen body is no more than the obverse of a fundamental dependence: the Spirit who makes the former into *koinonia* comes to it from this body of the Lord of glory.

b) *Per Lønning*, a Norwegian Lutheran at the Ecumenical Institute of the Lutheran World Federation in Strasbourg, was responsible for the follow-up address to Tillard's. After self-critical comments on the Lutheran confession and an explanation of the Lutheran view of the church using Article 7 of the Augsburg Confession, Lønning took up in the third part of his address what Tillard had said:

First what Father Tillard has presented seems to me to be a profound *biblical* description of churchliness — which is extremely important *per se*. But apart from perhaps three or four references to a terminology of the church as "sacrament" (which is not derived directly from the Bible), there is no reference in his paper to distinctively "Catholic" (in the meaning of Roman) ecclesiological features. His exegesis, therefore, provides no justification of Catholic ecclesiological claims, such as they have traditionally been propounded with the effect of disqualifying other churches. This I would be the last in the world to deplore. My observation is, however, that with the gratifying concord thus obtained we are not yet at the crucial point of confrontation. If this could mean that the traditional Roman claims, as far as they imply a disqualification of other churches, are given up in light of the biblical evidence, so much the better. But if these claims, or at least some of them, still persist, there remains a good deal of exegesis to be done before the biblical evidence, which should lead to a real exchange on the "problem within the problem", is on the table. What Father Tillard has presented is the "Catholic" view in the meaning of catholic, i.e. common to all Christians sharing the ecumenical credo. What might go beyond this, would obviously need a further justification.

My second question may seem to contrast a little with the first. I have put a question mark after the concept of the church as "*sacramentum*". I do this, however, not because I see this notion as necessarily delusive or as intended to introduce some aberrant understanding of the church, but because I wonder whether it is helpful. Does it really solve more problems than it creates? I doubt it . . .

Concerning the word "sacrament", it may cause some confusion that the church as such be conceptually placed on an equal footing with the sacraments given to, and administered by, the same church. It is also the case that the sign character of the sacraments is something given, constituted by the sacramental event of word and of visible elements, whereas the visible appearing of the church is constituted precisely by the sacraments as they are realized in literal practice. To speak of the church as "sacrament" may therefore easily obscure her character as receiver and as spender of *the* sacraments. It might also lead to equalizing the instituted givenness of bread and wine (just to illustrate my point by a concrete example) and the institutional givenness of church structures in general. For this reason I find this terminology a bit risky. It tends to introduce confusion more than to provide clarification.

To safeguard, underline and clarify the sign character of the church, I find a more helpful concept is that which Vancouver brought to the fore as its main contribution to theological reflection on unity, namely "*the eucharistic vision*". As far as I can see, all the substantial elements advocated — and rightly advocated — by Father Tillard are at least equally contained in that formula, and at the same time it is considerably better protected against institutionalistic misunderstandings. It is clear, namely, that here the essential, indispensable sign is the church, not as an institutional complex nor as a static structure, but as a live organism, visible in her central act of self-realization. The sacramentality of the church is none other than the sacramentality of her ministry, the proclamation of the gospel in word and in deed. As a Lutheran I could find no better way of phrasing this than by resorting to Father Tillard himself: "Here the eucharist appears as the *sacramentum par excellence* of the *koinonia*. It is at this point homogeneous with the church of God; the fathers will not hesitate to affirm that 'the eucharist constitutes the church'. In it is found all we have put forward. By receiving the eucharistic body and blood . . . the members of the celebrating community find themselves caught up in the very reality which fuses their *koinonia* together: the body whose members they are."

c) Speaking from a Caribbean perspective and also as a representative of the third world, *Horace Russell* discussed the marks of the church. It is striking how much closer to a concrete situation Russell is in tackling the unity, holiness, catholicity and apostolicity of the church. On unity he writes:

It was not until the 1930s (and the discussion gathered in strength until the 1950s) that the issues of unity and, with it, the "oneness" of the church arose. This was stimulated by the emergence of the Student Christian Movement in Jamaica and in the Latin islands which forced young people to take the unity of the church more seriously. And coeval with this movement within the church there emerged also a growing awareness of the unity of the region in political and economic terms. It is a great temptation to suggest that both events are inter-related but the evidence for this is scant. At the same time, however, it must be observed that there is and has always been a close tie between religion, religious expression and politics.

Despite the attempts at discussion, the Week of Prayer for Christian Unity held each January, united Bible studies, joint services, "oneness" meant essential denominational oneness either in one island or across the region. At most it meant an acceptance of other Christians as Christians when you got to know them. If there was an expression of "oneness" it was only as the church and the churches came together in councils or other joint agencies to face a common task . . .

Similarly, at the inauguration of the Caribbean Conference of Churches 1973 the greeting sent to the churches observed:

"We remind you, as we remind ourselves, and declare to all that our purpose and objective in this venture is clearly set forth in the preamble to our accepted constitution now fully in effect:

"We as the Christian people of Caribbean separated from each other by barriers of history, language, culture, class and distance, desire because of our common calling in Christ to join together in a regional fellowship of churches for inspiration, consultation and cooperative action. We are deeply concerned to promote the human liberation of our people and are committed to the achievement of social justice and the dignity of man in society. We desire to build up together our life in Christ and share our experience with the universal brotherhood of mankind".

The letter goes on to spell out five themes of concern viz work, worship, reconciliation, development and power . . .

It will be observed that both the Jamaica Council of Churches' experience and the Caribbean Conference of Churches' reports lay emphasis upon a unity (or solidarity) in the concrete situation, as the church (the churches) face the need to witness. The churches assume their "oneness" to be an inner "oneness" related to the life in Christ as Bishop Percival Gibson in his booklet "Christ for Jamaica" observed: "The New Testament uses the word church as referring not only to the universal Christian society but also to each local congregation, but it never uses the word church as referring to a diversity of Christian denominations. We are obliged to confess with shame that our denominational system is flatly contrary to the Spirit if not the letter of the New Testament. What we need today is to close our ranks and see how far we can cooperate in the name of our common Master Jesus Christ in the proclamation of the one gospel."

3. From the Chantilly discussion

a) It soon became clear that all taking part were able to accept the basic model of the church as the *body of Christ*. Beyond doubt, the fact that it is clearly anchored in the New Testament made this basic ecumenical consensus easier to achieve. Thus preference was given to an organic and conciliar view of the church rather than to static and hierarchical ideas.

b) It was not disputed that as always there exist *profound differences* among the churches. Lønning mentioned three points of controversy: the bishop of Rome as Peter's successor, the authority of ecumenical councils as against scripture and the appeal to divine ordinances on behalf of specific forms of the exercise of ministry in the church. In all three instances, significantly enough, questions of authority, not to say power, are involved. In New Testament times too there were also already differences in ecclesiological ideas, for instance between Paul and Peter; these are wholly compatible with the model of the body of Christ. In all today's points of difference it must always be asked how far the diversity is legitimate or how far it represents a factor that can divide the churches.

c) Finally, the unity of the body of Christ is sacramentally based in the *one eucharist*. The one table of the Lord, to which all are called, firmly fixes Christian unity in the centre of the faith and makes its visible realization a matter of urgency.

The eucharistic meeting together of Christians round the same table is therefore a priority. Only then can a full eucharistic vision of the church, such as was outlined for the first time at Vancouver,[4] take shape.

d) *Ecumenical unity* thus means communion of the many in their diversity within the one body of Christ through participation and sharing. It is not a deadening uniformity, but rather a live communion of all the baptized, that represents the visible unity of the churches: the priesthood of all believers. This idea of unity points to an ecclesiology which is democratically slanted and conciliar.

e) The unity of the churches through the communion of their members has *ethical and political implications.* All Christians are called upon to embrace the races and classes of the first, second and third worlds in the communion of a worldwide people of God consisting of Jews and Gentiles. As Moltmann explicated, there has to be a movement towards an ecumenical universality that will leave the imperialistic shadow of the past behind. This involves a departure from the West's claim to have the last word, and an opening up to new centres of Christendom in Africa, Asia and Latin America.

f) The ecumenical community is on the way to the kingdom of God; it is an *eschatological* community of God's pilgrim people. This insight is a safeguard for the ecumenical movement against inappropriate triumphalism.

4. The first draft explication

This consists of four parts. After the introduction on the local and the universal community the second part provides a Trinitarian development of the idea of the nature of the church as the people of God, the body of Christ and the communion of saints. Part three discusses the *eschatological* character of the church as a eucharistic community, as testifying by diakonia to God's active and transforming presence and also as prefiguring the kingdom of God. Finally, part four gives an interpretation of the four *notae ecclesiae*.[5]

5. Additions

The *Geneva* revised text again supported the explication with biblical and historical references. It related the *ekklesia* to the Old Testament *kahal*, clarified how the church related to humanity and highlighted the point that the church is rooted in the working of the Triune God:

> 1. The New Testament takes up and elaborates the Old Testament concept of a "chosen generation, a royal priesthood, a holy nation, a peculiar people", in applying it to the church and its calling to "show forth praises of him who has called it out of darkness into his marvellous light" (1 Pet. 2:5, 9; cf. Ex. 19:6), linking thus the *ekklesia* of the new covenant with its forerunner and model the *kahal* of the old. Both are chosen to serve in their turn as agents of God's will for humankind as a whole . . .
> . . .
> 3. In reflecting on the richness and life-giving power of the grace of God in Jesus Christ the primitive Christian community realized that this gift was not only for the salvation of individuals but was intimately connected with the destiny of humanity as a whole. For them what they called the "*church*" was that part of humanity seized by the creative and redemptive power of the Spirit of Christ. They also realized that it was through the preaching and witness of the Christian community that the good news of salvation was offered to all people till the end of time. It became clear to them that in this way the church was not only the community which confesses the faith but is also part of that confession (references).

4. It was, therefore, impossible for the *fathers* at Nicea and Constantinople to proclaim and confess the Triune God and his mighty acts in creation and redemption without proceeding from there to the church. Accordingly, the confession of Christ's cross and resurrection leads to the confession of the Holy Spirit who brings together and builds up the church on the foundation of the same redemptive act in cross and resurrection . . . (III, BI).

6. From the Stavanger discussion

a) Naturally enough, discussion of the church took most of the time available for the third article. All in all there was complete agreement on the community-related approach and its Trinitarian development. But various Western theologians were concerned that too much *independence* was being allowed to the church, and wanted reassurance that any impression of a fourth article of the Creed should be avoided: the church is wholly dependent on the Holy Spirit and no quality of independence attaches to it.

b) Against the background of the discussion on baptism, eucharist and ministry, more clarity was sought on the relation between *church and sacraments*. Is it the sacraments that constitute the church? Some participants had the impression that the Crêt-Bérard draft put too much emphasis on the eucharist and did not devote enough attention to baptism, whereas in the Nicene Creed it is the other way round.

c) At Stavanger it was stressed that it is not just the body of Christ as a whole that lives from the gifts of the Spirit, but also each individual one of its members. The charisms of the Spirit bestowed on each individual lead all in all to a stronger emphasis on the *priesthood of all believers*. The church is safeguarded in this way from clerical tutelage and the laity is allowed to have more say.

d) There was a reminder too in this context of the *ethical and social dimensions* of the church. It must be plain that, speaking horizontally, the church gives prophetic signs — is indeed itself a prophetic sign. It is in the local church that these effects should first become visible. For as Wolfhart Pannenberg (from Munich) says, the church catholic is present first and foremost in the local churches and not in a higher superstructure.

e) Opinion in Stavanger was that the *eschatological* character of the church ought also to be brought out more strongly. Here and now the church is already living in the experience of the future. For Orthodox theologians this view is of particular importance. Thomas Hopko and the Fitzgeralds from the USA have put it this way:

> Faith and Order speaks much about how the church is "not yet" the kingdom of God. We do not speak much — or clearly and emphatically enough — about how the church is "already" the kingdom.
> Therefore we need not only "references to the dialectical tension between the 'already' and 'not yet' of the kingdom". We *also* need greater clarity and precision and depth in regard to how the church is "already" the presence of the kingdom; how the church is one — and not divided; *holy* — and not sinful; *catholic* — and not fragmented; *apostolic* — and not unrooted or "charismatically wilful" . . .

7. On the Berlin/Potsdam explication

a) The *structural build-up* of the explication has been tightened. The introduction is now under the sub-title "The Church, Reflecting the Trinitarian Communion". This makes the context of the theological argument plain. The Trinitarian sequence of the explication is kept — people of God, body of Christ, communion of saints — and the eschatological elements are integrated with them. The interpretation of the marks of the church is a concise summary of what had previously been worked out.

b) As to content, the explication begins with the *Trinitarian anchoring* of the church: "According to the Creed, there is an indissoluble link between the work of God in Jesus Christ through the Holy Spirit and the reality of the church" (III, B.24). "The church has its origin, life and unity in the communion with the Trinity" (III, B.34). This should finally dispose of the danger of treating the church as an independent entity.

c) As the body of Christ, the church experiences its deepest reality in *eucharistic communion*. Here the eucharist is explicated non-sacramentally as the church's praise in the name of humanity and creation and as a call to all people for service (para. 41). Baptism is now allowed a section on its own, which was wholly absent from the Chantilly draft and only partially present in the Crêt-Bérard draft (§§58–62).

d) On the *priesthood of all believers* the text now runs: "The royal priesthood of all the faithful and the diverse ordained ministries serve God in the body of Christ by the Holy Spirit. The body of Christ thus reflects the active presence of the Trinity in the world" (para. 40). It may be asked whether these explanatory comments are in themselves enough to give force to the social and ethical dimension of the church as the body of Christ. At all events, the section of BEM dealing with "the Eucharist as communion of the faithful" does already go further.[6]

e) The explication of the *unity* of the church as a *communion* or fellowship within the one body of Christ continues to point the way foward. "The unity of all Christians needs to show itself visibly . . . , and this can be fully accomplished only in one eucharistic communion" (para. 47). The approach through *communio* with God, with each other, with humanity and with creation brings this ecumenical explication of the church astonishingly close to the *communio* ecclesiology as developed in Rome at the end of 1985 by the Roman Catholic Synod of Bishops.[7]

III. Living our hope

1. Approaches

After the "we believe", which is valid for all three articles, and the "we confess" as to the one baptism, the Creed goes on thirdly to "we look forward", to give expression to the Christian hope. For being a Christian means living in remembrance of the past, in recognition of the present and in hope for what is to come. To have an appropriate grasp of the present it is essential to be able to look towards the future and back into the past. As to content, the Creed addresses itself to two dimensions of Christian hope: the personal dimension, with the "resurrection of the dead" and the general one, with the "life of the world to come".

In principle, all the main Christian traditions are in agreement in their eschatological hope. Apart from differing views on points of detail, e.g. on the status of the dead, there are here — thank God! — no controversies of a fundamental nature, or such as would divide churches; not even between Christians and Jews. Nevertheless, all the Christian traditions, and the Protestant ones in particular, may well be none the worse for a broadening of their picture of the future — which is frequently restricted to individuals and to their own churches — so that they do not lose sight of the overall aim which is the life of the world to come in the kingdom of God.

Both within and outside the church there are those today who are all the more radical in calling in question the Christian hope. The big challenges with which now more than ever the Christian confession of hope has to contend range from a pervasive resignation and despair all the way to nihilism. What is at stake here is not simply the reason for the Christian hope and its content but rather its effects on our present-day life. How can we derive strength from hope in the last things for our life in the period that precedes them? How can the Christian hope for the future be communicated in such a way that life today is already transformed? From this eschatological angle the credibility of Christian transcendence comes most pressingly under scrutiny.

2. How contemporaries see it

It was unexpectedly difficult to find someone who could present a talk at Chantilly summarizing Christian eschatology. In the end *Ann Loades*, an Anglican who teaches in the Department of Theology at Durham, England, was willing at short notice to put together some views from New Testament and contemporary sources, to serve as an introduction to the discussion:

> Hope for the future of this world and for the life to come is not given much space in Western industrial and post-industrial culture; it does not enhance production or serve the glory of the state, for example, but it does raise difficult and worrying questions about the meaning of life, and where our trust ultimately lies.
>
> Our imaginations are filled with "worst-case scenarios". It is not easy to affirm the austere optimism that Christianity even at its most cautious and minimal invites us to embrace: to affirm, that is, the possibility of the reality that good can and will prevail over evil, or more precisely, that God brings good out of blackest evil, that there is a divine saving judgment for this world.
>
> See John 17:5 where Christ prays: "I pray not that thou shouldest take them out of the world, but that thou shouldest keep them from the evil." Looking at what happened to the person who prayed in that way, and to others who have staked their lives on the affirmation of certain absolute values, we see the cost of hope. To use Austin Farrer's words about Christ's death, it was a deprivation of life exacted by malice, accompanied by ignominy, executed with torture.[8] Christ became a self-offering put beyond the possibility of recall, nailed up alive, immovable, dragged through the breakdown of the body to the breaking of the mind, of which the last fragments and leavings were verses from the psalms.[9]
>
> Hope affirms that "God leaves no factors out of his reckoning, nor does he plan for an imaginary virtue we haven't got, he plans for the very men we are".[10] Hope believes in God's own act of self-justification. Almighty love gives his human creatures a vestige of his likeness, and "intervenes with incarnation and redemptive sacrifice to save them from natural perishableness and unnatural perversity".[11] If we can believe that God acts everywhere, by ceaseless creative energy and providential leading, we may also say "that he added this above all, that he totally identified himself with one of his physical creatures and personally acted in and by that creature's life".[12]
>
> The New Testament is in part responding to Psalms such as 115:15–18 and 116:1–9. Can the dead praise God as the dying man, and can we conceive of this without being too individualistic or anthropomorphic about it (see for example Rom. 8:19–21; 2 Pet. 3:2–13 and Rev. 21:1–6)? Whatever we say here, we have to acknowledge that language is being strained almost to breaking point. There are mysteries we cannot absolutely penetrate, whatever the language we use — of resurrection, immortality, eternal life, the communion of saints, the vision of God,

incorporation into Christ etc. The point is that if we are to talk of what God does to bring good out of blackest evil, it will be *mediated* through the metaphors and analogies we use to explain how we think about other people. If we do not get this right, our eschatological language will be even more of a problem . . . .

3. From the Chantilly discussion

On this theme five points in particular received special attention:

a) From 1971 till 1978 the Commission on Faith and Order carried out a seven-year study process which was rounded off at Bangalore in 1978 with the declaration entitled "A Common Account of Hope".[13] Chapters IV and VII, "Our Hope in God" and "Hope as the Invitation to Risk" broke new ground.

b) Christian hope has a personal and a community dimension. On the *personal* side, its slogan is "the resurrection of the dead". Here the hope is for the renewed gift of personal identity beyond death. This means looking squarely at death and not repressing the thought of death, for in the "resurrection of the dead" a limit is set to death. Finally, as Paul tells us in 1 Corinthians 15, even death is overcome, as the "last enemy", and is brought within God's creative power for life. Hence, as Frieda Haddad has said, even in the midst of the experience of death in Beirut, Job's confession holds good: "I know that my redeemer lives" (19:25).

c) It is particularly important to develop the *community* dimension of Christian hope, for that is a safeguard against narrowness and egocentricity. It includes remembrance of the "cloud of witnesses": all who died in Christ are gathered together into the communion of saints. It also includes the "subsumption" of human history into the celebration of the kingdom of God. But within this there is also the transformation of the earth and the cosmos in God's new creation. "The life of the world to come" will embrace not less but more than the transient world: it will embrace the whole creation, which will have attained to its fulfilment.

d) "The resurrection of the dead", "the communion of saints" and "the kingdom of God" are *metaphors*, word-pictures that attempt to express verbally the reality of God's future. As we are concerned here with a future sphere which is veiled from human experience, it is appropriate, and indeed necessary, to use analogical and metaphorical turns of speech. These give assurance about what is yet to come to people living today; they anticipate God's future in the power of hope, but they must be recognized as distinct from the realization of that future.

e) The Christian hope leads to a dynamic not of passive endurance but of active expectation. In the expectation of what is to come in what is already present there lies an attitude of *anticipation*. This shows itself both in acceptance of the present and opposition to it, and extends through ever-widening circles to mark out a path for hope in the midst of the sufferings of this present age.

4. The first draft "explication"

This has four parts:

I. The church as a communion of hope
II. Jesus Christ — the hope of the world
III. The oneness and wholeness of Christian hope
   a) kingdom of God
   b) resurrection
   c) new heaven and earth
IV. Living out our hope

5. Additions

The April 1985 *Geneva* revision prefixed to the concluding part on "living out our hope" a section which summarizes some "constitutive elements of the apostolic faith" and highlights them as adequate grounds for the "new perspective" in the midst of our world under threat:

> To believe in the life-giving and transforming power of the Holy Spirit, to be the *koinonia* of God's people in Christ's church, sent to all people to proclaim and live the good news of salvation until the end of history, to become through baptism for the forgiveness of sins partakers of the new life of the risen Lord and to receive thereby the assurance of sharing with all creation in the life of the world to come — all these are constitutive elements of the apostolic faith throughout the ages. They give Christians also today an unshakable foundation and new perspective for their involvement in the affairs of this world. This finds its central expression in our Christian hope in the midst of a threatened and finite world. (III, D.14).

6. From the Stavanger discussion

a) *As a whole* the explication of the Christian hope did not receive undivided approval. Study group 3 commented as follows on the Crêt-Bérard draft: "The final section on the life of the world to come is rather weak. The churches will want to understand that. Thus scriptural loci need to be given" (C.I, 6).

b) In connection with the kingdom of God it is noted that "*cosmic* transformation" is not sufficiently highlighted. Like personal resurrection it is to be seen as a consequence deriving from the death and resurrection of Christ. For the raising of Jesus Christ from the dead embraces equally the personal and the cosmic dimension.

c) The unqualified rejection of the idea of *restoration* (*apokatastasis*: "rejected by official doctrinal statements of all churches") is felt to be inappropriately brusque. The English-speaking theologian Martin Cressey commented that his own church in England, the United Reformed Church, had produced a doctrinal statement which leaves open some possibility of believing in universal salvation, even though it in no way endorses this.

d) As regards the consequences of Christian hope for life *today*, the opinion was expressed that the world to come is relegated too much to the future instead of being understood as God's future arriving in the present. "It is also possible to experience the world to come already in the present." The accent should lie on the consequences of Christian hope in the future for present-day life.

e) Finally, it was complained that the effects of Christian hope for the present were being developed only personally, socially and politically. "Yet the imagery of the eschaton — the banquet of the Lamb, the New Jerusalem, the vision of God — presents the *enjoyment of God* in the communion of saints as the fulfilment of our human destiny. Thus, our present participation in contemplative vision and joy in God is a further consequence of eschatological living" (ad. §74).

7. On the Berlin/Potsdam explication

This took up the Stavanger critique at least in three respects.

a) It stressed the *cosmic* dimension of hope in the kingdom of God in the sentence, "at the same time Christ's death and resurrection and the coming of the Spirit point forward to the final transformation of the cosmos" (III, C.II, para. 67).

b) The commentary on the question of *apokatastasis* (restoration) of all things is now made fuller and more open (in para. 69): it introduces the possibility of more positive reflection on the future of all human beings and things in the kingdom of God, beyond official ecclesiastical doctrinal statements which reject the idea:

> . . . Christian doctrine has to do justice both to the unlimited intention of God's saving love, but also to the many New Testament warnings that eternal damnation is possible. The tension between these different emphases in the biblical witness should not be dissolved by rationalizing one way or the other, but should be taken as indicating the openness of history.

c) *Joy* has now found its place among the aspects of Christian hope: "Our hope for this life and this world is grounded in, and will find its consummation in the vision and joy of God in the communion of saints" (para. 76).

Here too we may once again ask whether this explication adequately brings out the nature of Christian hope in the present life. There likewise remains much to be desired as regards the supporting biblical contexts. But the explication to date does make this much undoubtedly clear: we have a rich inheritance as regards the basis and content of Christian hope and this inheritance has latent in it the power to cope with the present challenges from our world under threat: *una fiducia — una caritas — unica spes*.[14]

NOTES

1. To date, the most far-reaching document relating to this rapprochment is the Klingenthal Memorandum compiled in the Commission on Faith and Order and entitled "The Filioque Clause in Ecumenical Perspective", in "Spirit of God, Spirit of Christ: Ecumenical Reflections on the *Filioque* controversy", L. Vischer ed., *Faith and Order Paper No. 103*, Geneva, WCC, 1981, pp.3–18. "Apostolic Faith Today: a Handbook for Study", H.-G. Link ed., *Faith and Order Paper No. 124*, Geneva, WCC, 1985, pp.231–244.
2. I use this term for simplicity and greater readability, *always* meaning the text of the Nicene-Constantinopolitan Creed of 381.
3. V. supra.
4. Cf. *Gathered for Life*, official report of the Sixth Assembly of the WCC, Vancouver 1983, David Gill ed., Geneva, WCC, 1983, pp.44f.
5. V. supra.
6. "Baptism, Eucharist and Ministry", *Faith and Order Paper No. 111*, Geneva, WCC, 1982, Eucharist para. 20, p.14.
7. Church — under the word — celebrates the mysteries of Christ — for the salvation of the world: esp. C. the church as "communio" and 7. ecumenical community.
8. *Saving Belief*, London, Hodder & Stoughton, 1964, p. 103.
9. *Lord I Believe*, London, SPCK, 1955, p. 93.
10. *Said or Sung*, Faith Press, 1960, p. 19.
11. *Faith and Logic*, ed. B. Mitchell, Allen & Unwin, 1957, p. 98.
12. *The Brink of Mystery*, ed. C. Conti, London, SPCK, 1976, pp. 109–110.
13. "Bangalore 1978: Sharing in One Hope", *Faith and Order Paper No. 92*, Geneva, WCC, 1978, pp.1–11. "Apostolic Faith Today", *op. cit.*, pp.84–92. The statement has the following sections: (I) thanksgiving; (II) voices of hope; (III) hopes encounter hopes; (IV) our hope in God; (V) the church: a communion of hope; (VI) shared hopes in the face of the common future; (VII) hope as the invitation to risk.
14. One faith — one love — sole hope.

Appendices

APPENDIX 1
The Participants

a) 14–22 November 1984, Kottayam, South India

Dr Roberta Bondi (United Methodist Church), Atlanta, USA

Rev. Janet Crawford (Church of the Province of New Zealand), Dunedin, New Zealand

Very Rev. Dr George Dragas (Ecumenical Patriarchate of Constantinople), Durham, England

Dr K.M. George (Orthodox Syrian Church of the East), Kottayam, Kerala, India

Metropolitan Paulos Mar Gregorios (Orthodox Syrian Church of the East), Kottayam, Kerala, India

Rev. Dr B.H. Jackaya (United Evangelical Lutheran Churches in India), Kusavankundi, Madurai, India

Rev. Dr O.V. Jathanna (Church of South India), Balmatta, Mangalore, India

Rev. Dr M.J. Joseph (Mar Thoma Syrian Church), Kottayam, Kerala, India

Ms Marianne Katoppo (Reformed Church), Jakarta, Indonesia

Fr Joseph Koikakudy (Roman Catholic Church), Kottayam, Kerala, India

Dr Ulrich Kühn (Federation of Evangelical Churches in the GDR: Lutheran), Vienna, Austria

Fr Jacob Kollaparambil (Roman Catholic Church), Kottayam, Kerala, India

Dr Moises Mendez (Baptist Convention), Mexico City, Mexico

Metropolitan Mar Osthathios (Orthodox Syrian Church), Kottayam, Kerala, India

Rev. Dr Rienzi Perera (Church of Sri Lanka), Pilimatalaw, Sri Lanka

Prof. Dietrich Ritschl (Evangelical Church in Germany: Reformed), Heidelberg, FRG

Prof. V.C. Samuel (Orthodox Syrian Church of the East), Bangalore, India

Miss Vimla Subaiya (Church of North India), Calcutta, India

Prof. Rowan Williams (Church of England), Cambridge, England

Faith and Order Secretariat

Rev. Dr Günther Gassmann (Evangelical Church in Germany: Lutheran)

Rev. Dr Hans-Georg Link (Evangelical Church in Germany: United)

Mrs Renate Sbeghen

b) 3–10 January 1985, Chantilly, France

Prof. Torleiv Austad (Church of Norway), Oslo, Norway

President Edward Czajko (United Evangelical Church), Warsaw, Poland

Prof. John Deschner (United Methodist Church), Dallas, USA

Dr Hermann Goltz (Federation of Evangelical Churches in the GDR: Lutheran), Halle, GDR

Ms Frieda Haddad (Greek Orthodox Patriarchate of Antioch and All the East), Beirut, Lebanon

Rev. Prof. Thomas Hopko (Orthodox Church in America), Tuckahoe, NY, USA

Prof. Sung-Hee Lee (Presbyterian Church of Korea), Taegu, Korea

Dr Ann L. Loades (Church of England), Durham, England

Prof. Per Lønning (Church of Norway), Strasbourg, France

Prof. Werner Löser (Roman Catholic Church), Frankfurt/Main, FRG

Prof. Nicolas Lossky (Patriarchate of Moscow), Paris, France

Dr Lauree Hersch Meyer (Church of the Brethren), Oak Brook, IL, USA

Prof. Jürgen Moltmann (Evangelical Church in Germany: Reformed), Tübingen, FRG

Rev. Dr M.F.G. Parmentier (Old Catholic Church), Hilversum, Holland

Prof. Janos D. Pasztor (Reformed Church in Hungary), Debrecen, Hungary

Rev. Michael Putney (Roman Catholic Church), Rome, Italy

Dr Michael Root (Lutheran Church in America), Columbia, SC, USA

Rev. Dr Horace O. Russell (Jamaica Baptist Union), Kingston, Jamaica

Ms Veronica Swai (Evangelical Lutheran Church in Tanzania), Moshi, Tanzania

Prof. Evangelos Theodorou (Church of Greece), Athens, Greece

Rev. Fr Jean M.R. Tillard (Roman Catholic Church), Ottawa, Canada

Dr Wolfgang Ullmann (Federation of Evangelical Churches in the GDR: Lutheran), Berlin, GDR

Prof. Livery Voronov (Russian Orthodox Church), Leningrad, USSR

Faith and Order Secretariat

Rev. Dr Günther Gassmann (Evangelical Church in Germany: Lutheran)

Rev. Dr Hans-Georg Link (Evangelical Church in Germany: United)

Mrs Renate Sbeghen

Frère Max Thurian (Reformed Church in France), Taizé, France

Vikar Dietrich Werner (coopted) (Evangelical Church in Germany: Lutheran), Oldenburg, FRG

c) 14–22 March 1985, Kinshasa, Zaire

Rev. Fr John K. A. Aniagwu (Roman Catholic Church), Ibadan, Nigeria

Dr Dan-Ilie Ciobotea (Romanian Orthodox Church), Bossey/Geneva, Switzerland

Prof. Sigurd Daecke (Evangelical Church in Germany: Lutheran), Aachen, FRG

Rev. Dr Efefe Elonda (Church of Christ in Zaire — Community of Disciples), Mbandaka, Zaire

Prof. Alasdair Heron (Church of Scotland), Erlangen, FRG

Fr Jonah Lwanga (Greek Orthodox Patriarchate of Alexandria), Nairobi, Kenya

Dr André Mampila (Roman Catholic Church), Kinshasa-Gombe, Zaire

Mgr Monsengwo Pasinya (Roman Catholic Church), Kisangani, Zaire

Rev. Dr Kjell Ove Nilsson (Church of Sweden), Uppsala, Sweden

Prof. Peder Nørgaard-Højen (Church of Denmark), Copenhagen, Denmark

Mrs Rosemary Nthamburi (Methodist Church), Nairobi, Kenya

Prof. Owango-Welo (Kimbanguist Church), Kinshasa, Zaire

Mrs Mary Tanner (Church of England), London, England

Prof. Günter Wagner (Baptist Church), Rüschlikon, ZH, Switzerland

Prof. Geoffrey Wainwright (Methodist Church of Great Britain), Durham, NC, USA

Dr Yemba Kekumba (Church of Christ in Zaire — Methodist Community), Kinshasa, Zaire

Faith and Order Secretariat

Rev. Dr Günther Gassmann (Evangelical Church in Germany: Lutheran)

Rev. Dr Hans-Georg Link (Evangelical Church in Germany: United)

Mrs Renate Sbeghen

Interpreters

Rev. Heinz Birchmeier, Geneva

Citizen Kampuna S., Kinshasa

APPENDIX 2
The Authors

Dr Dan-Ilie Ciobotea
Romanian Orthodox Church
Professor at the Ecumenical Institute Bossey
Céligny/Geneva, Switzerland

Rev. Dr Günther Gassmann
Evangelical Church in Germany: Lutheran
Director of the Secretariat of the Commission on Faith and Order
Geneva, Switzerland

Rev. Dr Hans-Georg Link
Evangelical Church in Germany: United
Executive Secretary in the Secretariat of the Commission on Faith and Order
Geneva, Switzerland

Prof. Dietrich Ritschl
Evangelical Church in Germany: Reformed
Professor of Systematic and Ecumenical Theology
Heidelberg, Federal Republic of Germany

APPENDIX 3

Faith and Order Publications on "Apostolic Faith Today"

"Towards a Confession of the Common Faith", P. Duprey and L. Vischer eds, *Faith and Order Paper No. 100, 1980*.

"Spirit of God, Spirit of Christ: Ecumenical Reflections on the Filioque Controversy", L. Vischer ed., *Faith and Order Paper No. 103, 1981*.

"Confessing Our Faith Around the World I", C.S. Song ed., *Faith and Order Paper No. 104, 1980*.

Does Chalcedon Divide or Unite? Towards Convergence in Orthodox Christology, P. Gregorios, W.H. Lazareth and N.A. Nissiotis eds, 1981.

"Towards Visible Unity. Commission on Faith and Order, Lima 1982. Vol. I: Minutes and Addresses", Section V: Towards the Common Expression of the Apostolic Faith Today, M. Kinnamon ed., *Faith and Order Paper No. 112, 1982*, pp.90–100.

"Towards Visible Unity. Commission on Faith and Order, Lima 1982. Vol. II: Study Papers and Reports", Part I: Towards the Common Expression of the Apostolic Faith Today, M. Kinnamon ed., *Faith and Order Paper No. 113, 1982*, pp.3–119.

"The Roots of Our Common Faith: Faith in the Scriptures and in the Early Church", H.-G. Link ed., *Faith and Order Paper No. 119, 1984*.

"Confessing Our Faith Around the World II", H.-G. Link ed., *Faith and Order Paper No. 120, 1983*.

"Confessing Our Faith Around the World III: the Caribbean and Central America", H.-G. Link ed., *Faith and Order Paper No. 123, 1984*.

"Apostolic Faith Today. A Handbook for Study", H.-G. Link ed., *Faith and Order Paper No. 124, 1985*.

"Confessing Our Faith Around the World IV: South America", H.-G. Link ed., *Faith and Order Paper No. 126, 1985*.